A voyage round

CHARLES DARWIN AND THE

THE UNIVERSITY OF CAMBRI

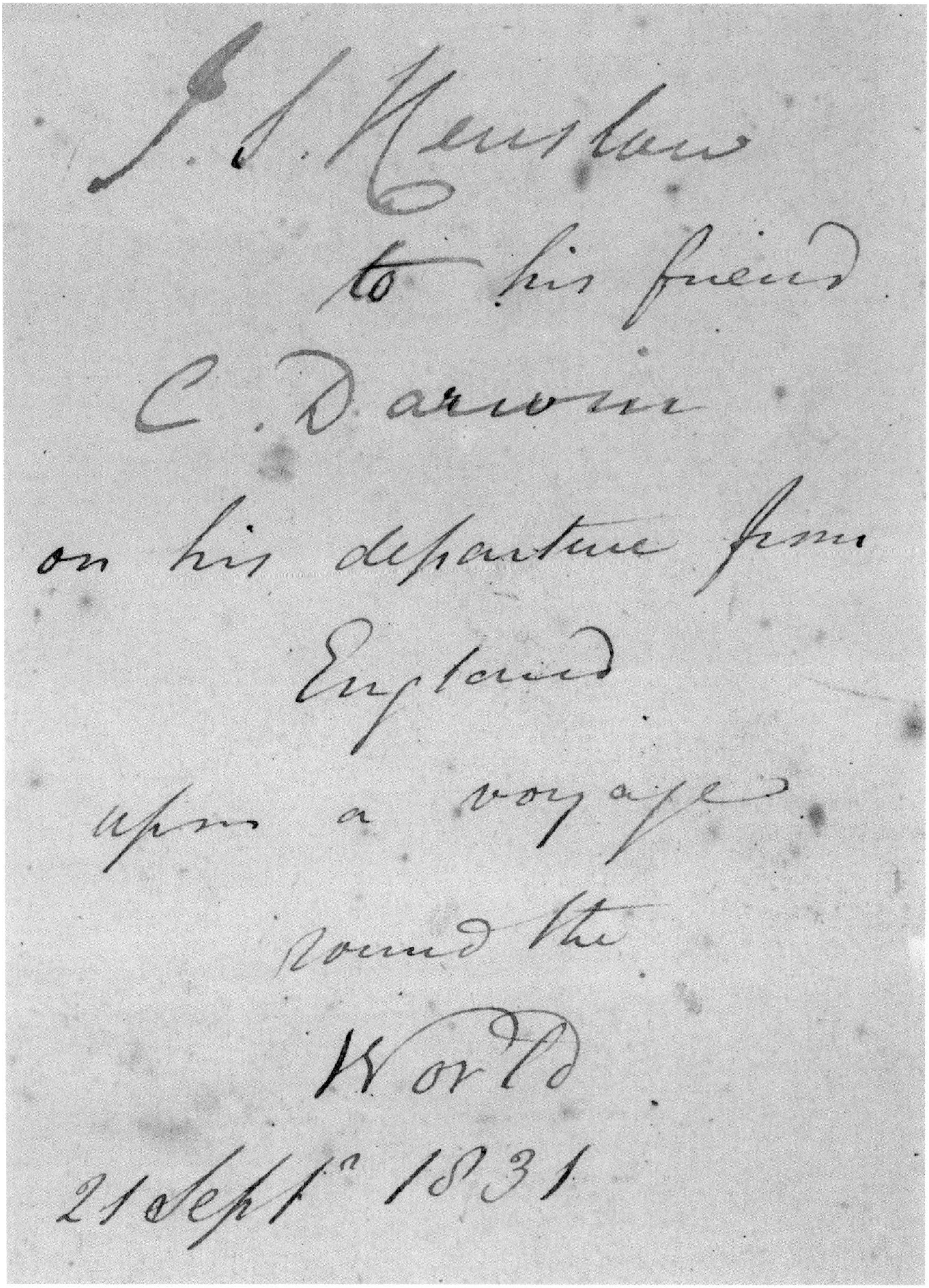

J. S. Henslow

 to his friend

C. Darwin

on his departure from

England

upon a voyage

round the

World

21 Sept.r 1831

Henslow's inscription in Humboldt's Personal Narrative, *given to Darwin just before the voyage*

A Voyage Round the World

CHARLES DARWIN AND THE BEAGLE COLLECTIONS IN THE UNIVERSITY OF CAMBRIDGE

Edited by
ALISON M. PEARN

CAMBRIDGE
UNIVERSITY PRESS

CAMBRIDGE UNIVERSITY PRESS
Cambridge, New York, Melbourne, Madrid, Cape Town, Singapore, São Paulo, Delhi, Dubai, Tokyo

Cambridge University Press
The Edinburgh Building, Cambridge CB2 8RU, UK

Published in the United States of America by Cambridge University Press, New York

www.cambridge.org
Information on this title: www.cambridge.org/9780521127202

First published 2009
Reprinted 2009

Printed in the United Kingdom at the University Press, Cambridge

A catalogue record for this publication is available from the British Library

ISBN   978–0–521–12720–2 paperback

Title page
Charles Darwin in 1839. Pencil sketch by George Richmond.

Contents

Foreword

RICHARD DARWIN KEYNES, FRS

Emeritus Professor of Physiology, University of Cambridge

This book is published in 'Darwin Year' – the 200th anniversary of his birth (1809) and the 150th anniversary of the publication of On the Origin of Species (1859) – to mark the particular connection between Charles Darwin and the University of Cambridge.

Darwin was an undergraduate at Christ's College from October 1827 until June 1831, and it was through friendships and interests developed in Cambridge during that period that he came to be offered the position of naturalist on HMS *Beagle*. Following his return from the voyage, in October 1836, Darwin lived for two or three months in Fitzwilliam Street, sorting through the specimens which he had sent back from distant parts to his Cambridge mentor, Professor Henslow. From 1842 until his death in 1882 Darwin lived at Down House, in the village of Downe, Kent; but he returned to Cambridge on several occasions, not least in order to visit three of his sons who had settled there.

The association between Darwin and Cambridge is explored further in this book. He wrote letters throughout the *Beagle* voyage to his immediate family, in Shrewsbury. He also wrote quite regularly to Professor Henslow, in a correspondence which symbolizes how important such sustained scientific exchanges would become to Darwin in later years, when working not from the *Beagle* but from his study, garden and greenhouse in Kent. Yet at the same time Darwin corresponded from the *Beagle* with several of his closest undergraduate friends, including his cousin, W. D. Fox (Christ's College), as well as J. M. Herbert (St John's), Charles Whitley (St John's) and Frederick Watkins (Emmanuel). One can see from these letters how much he liked to hear their news, and to remind himself of their 'snug breakfasts', and of beetle-hunting on the banks of the river Cam. Appropriately, the letters to Fox now form part of the archival material at Christ's College, alongside other traces of Darwin's undergraduate life in the late 1820s and early 1830s.

Many years later, in 1927, members of the Darwin family decided that Down House should be preserved as a memorial to Charles Darwin, and began to return furniture and other items which had been dispersed among them. Darwin's books and papers had also been dispersed; but it was not until the early 1940s that further steps were taken to settle their future. It was decided that the principal *Beagle* records (Darwin's field notebooks, the journal he kept throughout the voyage, and the letters sent home to his family) should pass to Down House, along with other *Beagle* relics, so that they could form part of an exhibition for the public. The bulk of Darwin's personal and scientific papers (including the quantity of geological, zoological and ornithological notes made on the *Beagle*) passed to Cambridge University Library, and have been supplemented there by further donations of related material, so that an archive has been created which is now the power house of the so-called 'Darwin Industry'. The library has also acquired other relevant items, including two of the sketchbooks used by Conrad Martens while serving as official artist on the *Beagle* from November 1833 to November 1834, and an important series of letters written from the *Beagle* by Captain FitzRoy to his sister Fanny. Collections of this quality need vision, scholarship and resources to make them better understood and more widely accessible; and for over 30 years the Darwin Correspondence Project, based in the University Library, but operating with the support of many other bodies, has been producing the magnificent volumes of Darwin's collected correspondence, on which the modern perception of the scientist at work must now depend.

There could, however, be nothing more immediately evocative of the *Beagle* voyage than the specimens carefully packed by Darwin, and his assistant Syms Covington, in caskets, barrels, jars, cigar-boxes and pill-boxes, and then shipped back to Professor Henslow in Cambridge. The specimens have come to rest in many different places. There are (for example) *Beagle* crabs in the University Museum of Natural History at Oxford, *Beagle* mockingbirds and finches in the Natural History Museum at Tring in Hertfordshire, and *Beagle* beetles, barnacles, spiders and fossils (of various kinds) in the Natural History Museum in South Kensington. In Cambridge, there are *Beagle* minerals, and more fossils, in the Sedgwick Museum of Earth Sciences, *Beagle* plants in the Herbarium of the Botany School, and *Beagle* beetles and fish in the University Museum of Zoology. Full use is made here of this wide range of material, and one cannot fail to be moved by all that it signifies for the development of man's understanding of the natural world.

In November 1877, Darwin returned to Cambridge in order to receive an honorary doctorate. The undergraduates crammed into the galleries on either side of the Senate House, famously contributing to the occasion by swinging a monkey on strings from one gallery to the other (not to mention a large iron ring, adorned with ribbons, to represent the 'missing link'), and cheering loudly when the public orator happened to use the word *apes* (Latin for 'bees') in his address. My grandfather John Neville Keynes, at that time a recently-elected fellow of Pembroke College (and some years later Registrary of the University), was present in the Senate House and described the event in his diary. 'Darwin bore himself in a rather trying position with remarkable dignity; but I heard afterwards that his hand shook so much while he was signing the registry, that his signature was scarcely legible.' Darwin's hand could verge on the illegible at the best of times; but it is to be hoped that the publication of this book, among the many other events occurring here and elsewhere in 2009, will reassure Darwin that his work is now taken seriously in Cambridge, and that his message has endured.

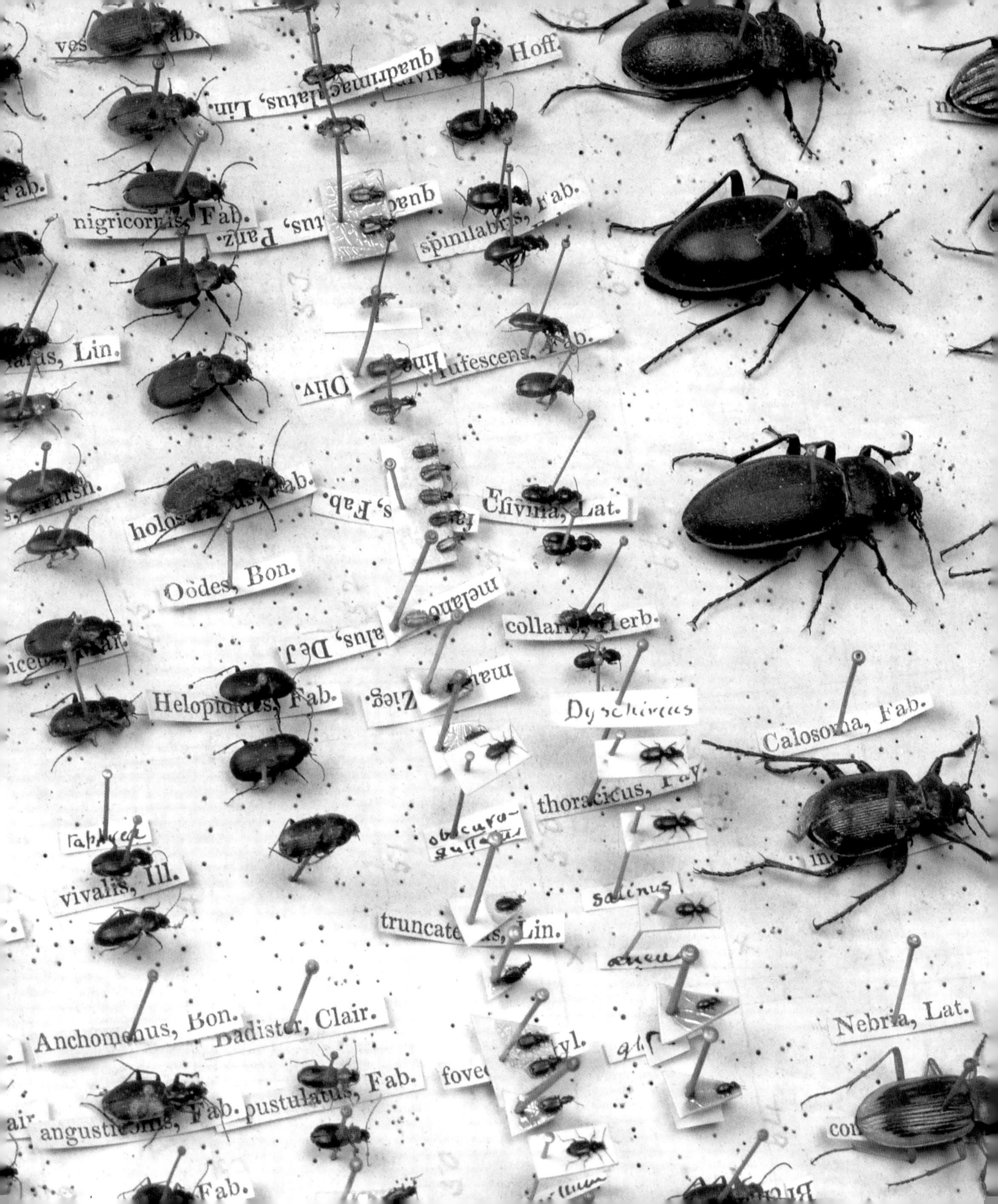

nigricornis, Fab.
spinilabris, Fab.
Clivina, Lat.
Oodes, Bon.
Dyschirius
Calosoma, Fab.
vivalis, Ill.
Anchomenus, Bon.
Badister, Clair.
Nebria, Lat.
pustulatus, Fab.

All idle men and entomologists

The twenty-two year old Charles Darwin was as relieved as any other student to hear in January 1831 that he had got successfully through his final exams. 'A man may be excused, for writing so much about himself', he crowed in a letter to his cousin, William Darwin Fox, 'when he has just passed the examination'.

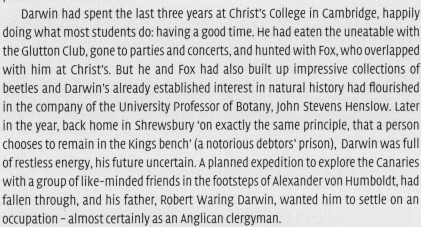

Darwin had spent the last three years at Christ's College in Cambridge, happily doing what most students do: having a good time. He had eaten the uneatable with the Glutton Club, gone to parties and concerts, and hunted with Fox, who overlapped with him at Christ's. But he and Fox had also built up impressive collections of beetles and Darwin's already established interest in natural history had flourished in the company of the University Professor of Botany, John Stevens Henslow. Later in the year, back home in Shrewsbury 'on exactly the same principle, that a person chooses to remain in the Kings bench' (a notorious debtors' prison), Darwin was full of restless energy, his future uncertain. A planned expedition to explore the Canaries with a group of like-minded friends in the footsteps of Alexander von Humboldt, had fallen through, and his father, Robert Waring Darwin, wanted him to settle on an occupation – almost certainly as an Anglican clergyman.

In what seemed his last weeks of freedom, Darwin joined another of his Cambridge teachers, the geologist Adam Sedgwick, on a field trip in the Welsh mountains. When he got back to Shrewsbury on 29 August his sisters were full of excitement: there was a letter waiting for him. Henslow had put Charles's name forward for a place on an Admiralty surveying voyage to South America as captain's companion on-board HMS *Beagle*. Darwin was not the first choice: Henslow had briefly considered accepting the place himself, and had then asked his brother-in-law, Leonard Jenyns (who was later to work on Darwin's collection of fish specimens), but both men had young families as well as careers and were forced to turn it down.

Beginnings

When Darwin arrived at Cambridge his taste for natural history was already established. During his brief time as a medical student in Edinburgh he had studied the plants and animals of the sea and shore, and even given a talk on the results of his research. At Cambridge he was exposed to a circle of active fellow students and teachers, men such as Adam Sedgwick, John Stevens Henslow, and Leonard Jenyns, all of whom inspired Darwin not only while he was at Cambridge, but during and after the *Beagle* voyage. And he read: books, in particular those of Alexander von Humboldt, Charles Lyell, and John Herschel, played a major part in Darwin's developing scientific understanding. He also developed his social skills, and it was Darwin's ability to get on well with other people as much as his scientific qualifications, that equipped him for a place on board.

JOHN PARKER

Darwin and Henslow

In his *Autobiography* Darwin makes a very hard judgement on himself, claiming that the three years he spent at Cambridge were 'wasted'. These same years, however, were immensely formative and without them we would not have seen the unfolding and flowering of his remarkable genius. He came to Cambridge to read for a degree to enable him to become a clergyman but, apart from a few compulsory ones in his college, as an undergraduate he attended just one course of lectures, those of John Stevens Henslow, Professor of Botany, which he found were 'universally popular and as clear as daylight'. Darwin first took Henslow's botany course in the summer of 1829, and then was drawn back again in 1830 and 1831.

❝ As to what I have been & am now doing, the less that is said about it, the better: my time is solely occupied in riding & Entomologizing. ❞
To W. D. Fox [18 May 1829]

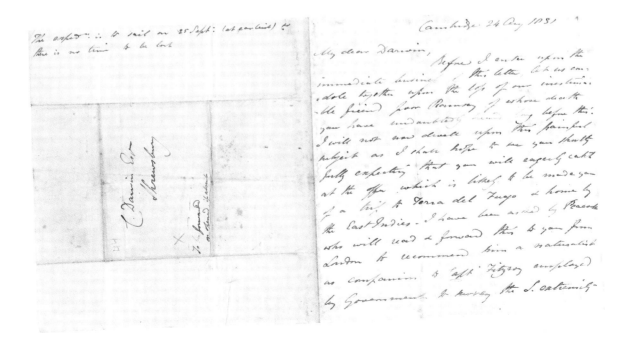

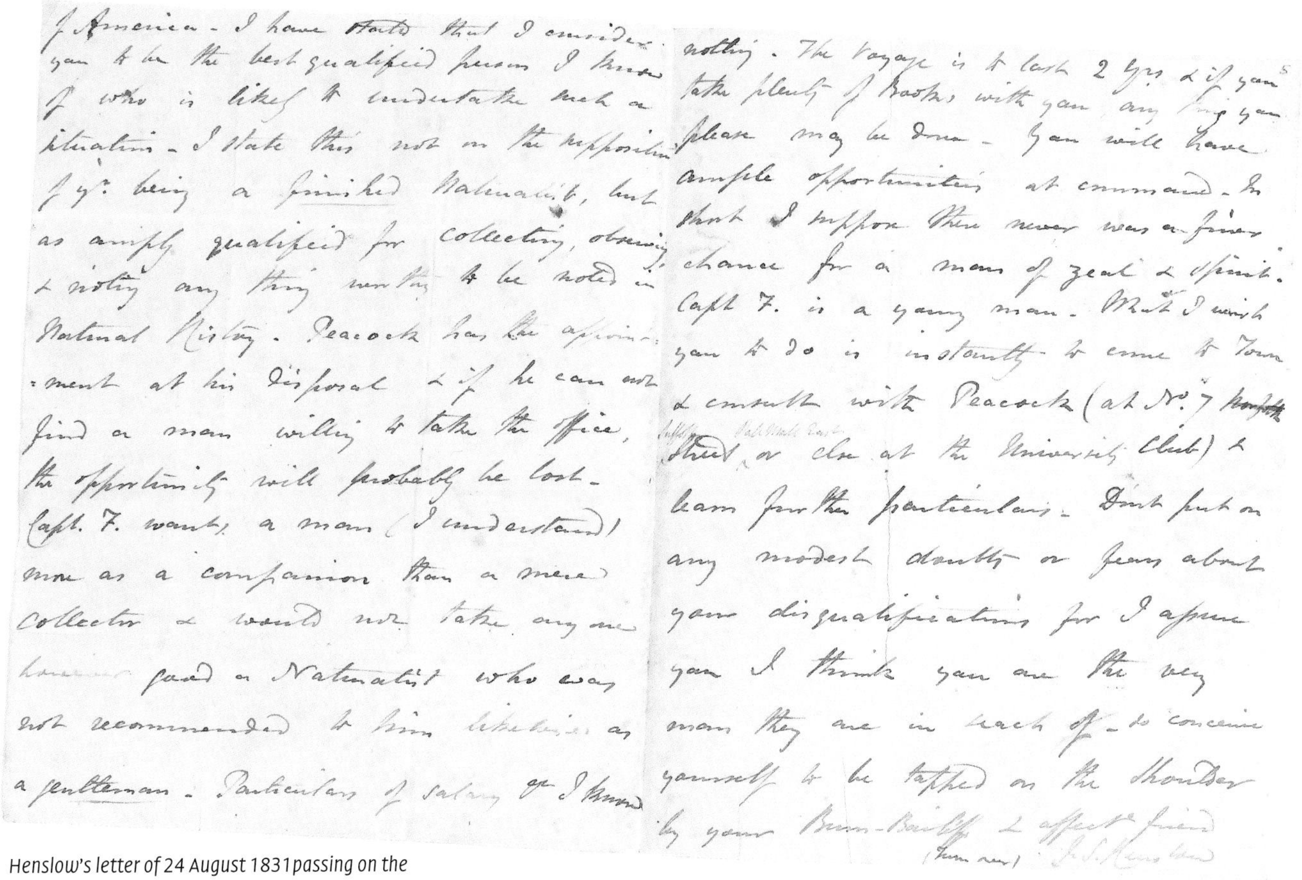
of America - I have stated that I consider you to be the best qualified person I know of who is likely to undertake such a situation - I state this not on the supposition of yr. being a finished Naturalist, but as amply qualified for collecting, observing & noting any thing worthy to be noted in Natural History. Peacock has the appointment at his disposal & if he can not find a man willing to take the office, the opportunity will probably be lost - Capt. F. wants a man (I understand) more as a companion than a mere collector & would not take any one however good a Naturalist who was not recommended to him likewise as a gentleman. Particulars of salary &c I know

nothing. The voyage is to last 2 yrs. & if you take plenty of Books with you, any thing you please may be done - You will have ample opportunities at command - In short I suppose there never was a finer chance for a man of zeal & spirit. Capt F. is a young man. What I wish you to do is instantly to come to Town & consult with Peacock (at No. 7 ~~Suffolk~~ Suffolk Pall Mall East Street, or else at the University Club) & learn further particulars. Don't put on any modest doubts or fears about your disqualifications for I assure you I think you are the very man they are in search of - so conceive yourself to be tapped on the shoulder by your Bum-Bailiff & affect. friend

(turn over) J. S. Henslow

Henslow's letter of 24 August 1831 passing on the offer of a place on board HMS Beagle: 'I assure you I think you are the very man they are in search of'.

John Stevens Henslow (1796–1861)

From his earliest years, John Stevens Henslow was fascinated by the natural world. As a schoolboy he assisted in cataloguing the zoological collections of the British Museum; as a student in Cambridge he discovered a new species of freshwater snail, named after him, and began a life-long friendship with Adam Sedgwick, Professor of Geology, who introduced him to field studies. In 1819 Henslow carried out a field survey of the Isle of Man, and two years later made a comprehensive study of the geology of the island of Anglesey. He launched his plant collecting quite suddenly in March 1821, and by the end of the year had collected 263 flowering plants. In 1822, Henslow was appointed Professor of Mineralogy, and, less than three years later, at the age of 29, was also awarded the Chair of Botany. He resigned the Chair of Mineralogy in 1827, but remained Professor of Botany until his death in 1861. Henslow was curate of Little St Mary's Church, Cambridge, from 1824 to 1832, then vicar of Cholsey-cum-Moulsford, Berkshire, and finally rector of Hitcham, Suffolk, from 1837, a post he also held until his death. As Professor of Botany he successfully campaigned for a new and much larger site for the Cambridge University Botanic Garden.

JP

John Stevens Henslow

Henslow's botany classes

From his appointment to the Chair of Botany, Henslow worked strenuously to establish botany as an esteemed science in the University. He had inherited little of use in teaching from his predecessor, who had allowed the Herbarium to decay and had neglected the Botanic Garden. He set about producing seventy impressive elephant folio illustrations to use in his lectures, and amassed a huge teaching collection of botanical illustrations. He also began immediately to agitate for a new, much larger, botanic garden to hold a collection of trees, shrubs, and herbs suitable for the study of 'physiological botany'.

Henslow published a brief syllabus of his lecture course in 1828: it took place in the Easter term, occupying five weeks from April to early June. As well as lectures, Henslow's students were given practical sessions in which a huge variety of different plants were presented to them for dissection. In Darwin's first course in 1829, he handled 268 different plants. Highly enjoyable, too, were the regular outings around Cambridge during which Henslow expounded on everything of interest they came across, whether flower, toad, snail, or rock.

Students found Henslow's lucid teaching very engaging, and the man himself very approachable. Darwin was drawn into his circle, invited to join Henslow's weekly soirées where he obtained privileged insights into the issues of current concern in the natural sciences.

Henslow's botanical research

The dynamism of Henslow's research can be established from the extraordinary range of topics covered in his publications, which reach their peak numbers between 1829 and 1832. His papers during these critical years, when Darwin attended his botanical course, concern: hybridisation and species identity in *Primula*, *Digitalis* and *Anagallis*; variation in the number of parts of flowers in *Paris*; 'monstrous' forms of flowers; the nature of reproduction in *Chara* (fresh-water algae); plant biogeography; and even three zoological contributions on snakes, birds and jellyfish. Foreshadowing Darwin, too, was Henslow's use of his own garden in Cambridge for experiments and observations.

Henslow addressed the nature of species by examining the extent and importance of variation in nature, the role of 'monstrosity' as a key to understanding the developmental laws that govern nature, and the importance of hybridisation as a way of determining the limits of species. Indeed, Henslow was obsessed by variation, and Darwin arguably gained this essential underpinning for his own thoughts from his deep intimacy with Henslow. This was an influence which lasted until Henslow's death in 1861, soon after the publication of the *Origin of Species* and just at the beginning of Darwin's own botanical outpourings.

> " I have been asked by Peacock . . . to recommend him a naturalist as companion to Capt Fitzroy employed by Government to survey the S. extremity of America – I have stated that I consider you to be the best qualified person I know of who is likely to undertake such a situation – I state this not on the supposition of yr. being a finished Naturalist, but as amply qualified for collecting, observing, & noting any thing worthy to be noted in Natural History. "
> Henslow to Darwin, 24 August 1831
> (see pp. 10-11)

An avenue of pines in Cambridge University Botanic Garden planted by Henslow to show variation.

> " I owe more than I can express to this excellent man ... . I was strongly attached to natural history, and this attachment I owed, in large part, to him. "
> Charles Darwin on John Stevens Henslow

Darwin and Humboldt

ALISTAIR SPONSEL

The phases of Charles Darwin's career have often been defined by the books that he read, from Lyell's *Principles of Geology* during the *Beagle* voyage to Malthus's *Essay on the Principle of Population* during his London years. The book that encouraged him to pursue a scientific voyage in the first place was the *Personal Narrative* of Alexander von Humboldt's travels in Central and South America between 1799 and 1804.

When Darwin was a student at Christ's College, Humboldt's *Personal Narrative* fuelled his first truly grand ambitions. He was captivated by Humboldt's descriptions of the tropics, which he recited aloud to John Stevens Henslow and his friends while they were examining plants and turning over rocks on their rambles between Cambridge and Grantchester. So strong was Darwin's desire to emulate Humboldt that after taking his degree he started new studies of Spanish and geology, and began to plan a natural history excursion to Tenerife, where Humboldt had stopped on his passage to the Americas. He only finally set those plans aside when he was presented with the opportunity to join the *Beagle*.

The documents of the exciting autumn of 1831 prove that almost everyone in Darwin's circle considered Humboldt the ideal role model of a gentleman voyager. Adam Sedgwick advised Darwin that 'Humboldt's personal narrative you will of course get – He will at least show the right spirit with which a man should set to work.' A week later Darwin received his own copy of the English translation of the *Personal Narrative*, a gift from Henslow inscribed 'to his friend C. Darwin on his departure from England. upon a voyage round the World.' It was a talisman that no philosophically inclined traveller could afford to be without. As FitzRoy told Darwin while they were prioritising the items to be squeezed into their small *Beagle* cabins, 'You are of course welcome to take your Humboldt ... but, I cannot consent to leaving mine behind.'

Darwin's *Beagle* manuscripts reveal that he absorbed much more from Humboldt than an industrious spirit and a Romantic conception of nature. He used the *Personal Narrative* and Humboldt's writings on Asia as omnipresent sources of facts about topics as varied as the migration of birds, the average slope of a volcanic cone, the temperatures of seawater, the hibernation of crocodiles, and the geography and mineralogy of locations from the Cordillera to Central Asia. A review of the citations given in the 'little notebooks' that Darwin filled on the voyage and after suggests that Humboldt's influence on Darwin's thought was eclipsed only by that of Darwin's father and Charles Lyell. Less obvious, but no less profound, are the concepts and theories that Darwin learned from Humboldt's works and applied for himself. Darwin's oft-expressed obsession with the distribution of plants and animals, for example, and his fascination with the altitude (and submarine depth) where he found his specimens, echoed themes so central to Humboldt's work that a citation would have been redundant.

In its style, its subject matter, and its many references to the 'illustrious traveller,'

> " *Probably from reading so much of Humboldt, [you have] got his phraseology & ... without perceiving it got to embody your ideas in his poetical language.* "
>
> Caroline Darwin to Charles Darwin on reading the diary of his voyage

'J. S. Henslow to his friend C. Darwin on his departure from England upon a voyage round the World 21 Sept 1831'. Inscription inside the first volume of a set of Alexander von Humboldt's Personal Narrative *given to Darwin by John Stevens Henslow when Darwin visited him in Cambridge shortly before the Beagle sailed. The books went all round the world with Darwin, and he kept them for the rest of his life. They are now in the Darwin collection in Cambridge University Library.*

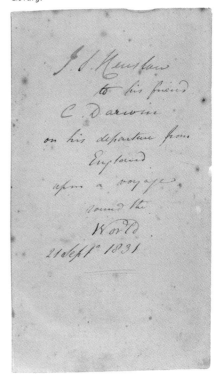

Alexander von Humboldt (1769-1859)

Alexander von Humboldt was a well-born Prussian exponent of a science of earth and life that he called 'Physique générale'. He was a friend and collaborator of Goethe and his associates in the German Romantic literary and scientific movement, and trained with Abraham Gottlob Werner, Europe's leading practitioner of mineralogy and geognosy. After working for half a decade as a mining engineer, Humboldt used the wealth from his parents' estate to finance a five-year trip to the Spanish Americas, where he and his companion Aimé Bonpland scaled the Andes, explored the Orinoco River, and accumulated an enormous mass of data through the enthusiastic use of a staggering load of scientific instruments carried by their porters. Upon returning to Europe in 1804, Humboldt settled in Paris. The expedition generated an endless stream of publications in which Humboldt compiled, analysed, and represented that data in tables and distribution maps alongside prose that urged an aesthetic appreciation of nature.   A S

In 1839 Darwin sent a copy of *Journal of Researches*, his popular account of the *Beagle* voyage, to Alexander von Humboldt, and was deeply moved to get this long and enthusiastic letter in reply. Humboldt, writing in French, told Darwin that he was proud to have inspired his work.

the published version of Darwin's diary, his *Journal* of the voyage, was a tribute to Humboldt's *Personnel Narrative*. Humboldt repaid this compliment with a letter that Darwin prized as much as any he ever received. 'You told me,' Humboldt wrote, 'that, when you were young, the manner in which I studied and depicted nature in the torrid zones contributed toward exciting in you the ardour and desire to travel in distant lands. Considering the importance of your work, Sir, this may be the greatest success that my humble work could bring. Works are of value only if they give rise to better ones.'

Humboldt died in 1859, six months before Darwin's *Origin of Species* was published. The Cambridge collection holds what might be considered Darwin's epitaph for his hero, written in a letter to another old voyager the year before Darwin's own death. 'I believe that you are fully right in calling Humboldt the greatest scientific traveller who ever lived,' Darwin told his friend Joseph Hooker. 'You might truly call him the parent of a grand progeny of scientific travellers, who taken together have done much for science.'

> 66 *I have long had a wish of seeing Tropical scenery and vegetation: & according to Humboldt Teneriffe is a very pretty specimen.* 99
> To W. D. Fox, 7 April 1831

Adam Sedgwick (1785–1873)

Adam Sedgwick was Woodwardian Professor of Geology at Cambridge University for more than fifty years from 1818 until his death. During most of that time he was also prebendary of Norwich Cathedral and a Fellow of Trinity College, Cambridge. With Roderick Impey Murchison, he was responsible for first identifying the Devonian geological time period; Sedgwick, following extensive fieldwork in Wales, also controversially proposed a Cambrian period older than Murchison's Silurian system. Darwin first attended Sedgwick's popular geology lectures in the months after his graduation and was invited to join him on one of his Welsh expeditions. The two men remained friends to the end of Sedgwick's life despite Sedgwick's later disapproval of Darwin's theory of natural selection.

It was Sedgwick who worked on most of Darwin's geological specimens from the *Beagle* voyage, and whose reading of Darwin's letters at meetings of the Geological Society of London helped establish Darwin's reputation as a geologist before the voyage was even ended. Sedgwick held a generally catastrophist view of the geological history of the earth and did not fully accept Charles Lyell's proposition that all observed phenomena could be explained by slow and gradual change.

Two of the rock samples collected by Adam Sedgwick during his field trip to Wales with Darwin in August 1831.

The memorial stone in the Dales village of Dent – Sedgwick's birthplace

Christ's College, Cambridge: The Darwin material

CANDACE GUITE

Charles Darwin arrived in Christ's College as a student in 1827 and the College archive still preserves unique records of his time there.

Darwin in the Old Library

Charles Darwin's name appears in the College Admissions Book for October 1827, there are copies of the College Examination papers he sat – and we even know what he ate. The daily bills of fare show that breakfast, for example, was a meal often shared with his cousin William Darwin Fox, also at Christ's; their student companionship marked the beginning of a life-long friendship and correspondence.

The most important part of the manuscript collection is a series of 156 letters Darwin addressed from Christ's College, most of them written to Fox. Beetles were a frequent topic of their correspondence; the letters known as Fox 1 and 2, include charming sketches of his prize specimens drawn for Darwin by one of his sisters. This remarkable collection of letters came into the possession of the College in 1909, a generous gift from Fox's grandson, in the centenary year of Darwin's birth.

Christ's Old Library holds copies of Darwin's publications, many in first editions, and much important secondary material, including a set of Russian translations, and material donated by the Moscow State Darwin Museum in 1959. The David Stanbury collection bequeathed in 1998 preserves unpublished research material relating to the *Beagle* voyage, Stanbury's own research library, and a rich visual archive containing reproductions of the work of *Beagle* artist Conrad Martens.

Detail of a letter from Darwin to his cousin, William Darwin Fox, in June 1828. The beetle sketches were done for him by one of his sisters.

Darwin's entry in Christ's College Admissions Book

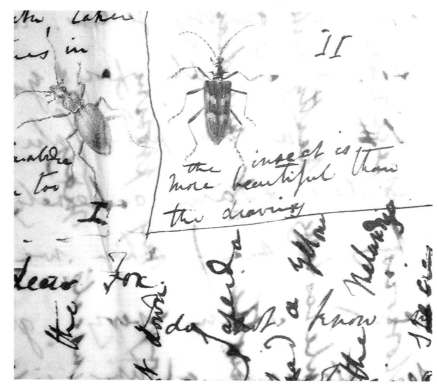

William Darwin Fox (1805–1880)

Charles Darwin's cousin, William Darwin Fox, was admitted to Christ's College on 26 January 1824. His tutor was Mr Shaw. He took his BA in 1829, and his MA in 1833, became an Anglican clergyman, and from 1838 to 1873 was Rector of Delamere in Cheshire. A keen amateur entomologist, Fox introduced Charles, with whom he overlapped at Christ's for six months, to his passion for beetles, and his own well established circle of friends, including John Stevens Henslow. Fox's diary and accounts for 1824 to 1826, on display in Christ's College Old Library, provide a delightfully direct and vivid account of student life at the time. Fox and Darwin corresponded throughout their lives.

The beetle Darwin couldn't bear to lose

A beetle that once got away from Charles Darwin and seemed to have disappeared from Cambridgeshire forever was rediscovered in Wicken Fen in 2008 after an absence of more than fifty years.

As a student at Cambridge, one of Darwin's favourite activities was beetle collecting, and the Crucifix Ground Beetle was one of the greatest prizes for a collector. Darwin told the story of trying to hold on to three beetles – one in each hand and one in his mouth – in a letter to his friend Leonard Jenyns in 1846.

'I must tell you what happened to me on the banks of the Cam in my early entomological days; under a piece of bark I found two Carabi (I forget which) & caught one in each hand, when lo & behold I saw a sacred Panagæus crux major; I could not bear to give up either of my Carabi, & to lose Panagæus was out of the question, so that in despair I gently seized one of the Carabi between my teeth, when to my unspeakable disgust & pain the little inconsiderate beast squirted his acid down my throat & I lost both Carabi & Panagæus!'

Darwin's Room and the Darwin Garden

Following recent research, Darwin's old room in Christ's, G4, has been restored and furnished appropriately to provide a glimpse of his College life. Some of the set texts required for his degree mingle with entomological works, a tiny pocket-sized edition of Milton's *Paradise Lost*, experiments with taxidermy and mineralogy, and the collecting paraphernalia of keen nineteenth century amateur entomologist.

The student Darwin is also to be found in the 'Darwin Garden' in the striking life size bronze commissioned by the College from sculptor Anthony Smith, a Christ's zoology graduate. The garden itself has been planted with species encountered by Darwin on the *Beagle* voyage.

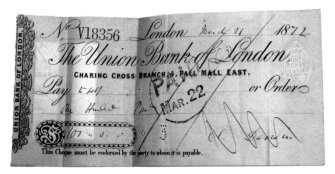

An unexpected discovery was made when a photographic portrait of Darwin hanging in the Old Library in Christ's College, was taken out of its frame: the autograph signature that appeared beneath the portrait was discovered to be the endorsed reverse of a cheque for £100 – a substantial amount of money at the time – made out by Darwin to 'self' and dated 21 March 1872. The portrait itself was taken around 1855 by the commercial photographers Maull and Polyblank for the Literary and Scientific Portrait Club.

Whirled around the world in a Ten Gun Brig

*Shrewsbury, Cambridge and London,
August – December 1831*

Slinging the monkey

For the next few months after Henslow's letter arrived, Darwin was in a fever of excitement, alternately euphoric at the prospect of adventure, or in despair that his reluctant father would finally veto the expedition, or that he would get permission only to find the place on the *Beagle* had been given to someone else. His letters show him dashing around the country from Shropshire to London, from London to Cambridge, where he breathlessly reported on progress to Henslow, and back to Shropshire. Then round again.

Darwin's uncle, Josiah Wedgwood, was drafted in as support and finally persuaded Robert Waring Darwin, already paying off Charles's student debts, to continue to bankroll his son for the planned two years of what must have appeared to any parent a long and potentially dangerous voyage. Darwin met the *Beagle*'s captain, Robert FitzRoy, and they were instantly pleased with one another. He said his goodbyes to his family and friends, and on 27 December 1831, after some delays in refitting the ship and a couple of false starts, the little *Beagle* and her crew of 74 finally sailed out of Plymouth harbour.

HMS Beagle, and the smaller Adventure, off Port Desire, Patagonia, by Conrad Martens. Captain FitzRoy annotated the sketch: 'Note Mainmast of the *Beagle* a little farthur aft. Miz. Mast to rake more.'

Getting permission

" Dear Wedgwood … Charles will tell you of the offer he has had made to him of going for a voyage of discovery for 2 years. – I strongly object to it on various grounds, but I will not detail my reasons that he may have your unbiassed opinion on the subject, & if you think differently from me I shall wish him to follow your advice.
Yours affectionately, R W Darwin Wednesday 31. "

Robert Waring Darwin,
Charles Darwin's father, to
his brother-in-law,
Josiah Wedgwood II,
30 and 31 August 1831

" My dear Father, … I have given Uncle Jos, what I fervently trust is an accurate & full list of your objections, & he is kind enough to give his opinion on all. – The list & his answers will be enclosed. – But may I beg of you one favor. it will be doing me the greatest kindness, if you will send me a decided answer, yes or no. – If the latter, I should be most ungrateful if I did not implicitly yield to your better judgement & to the kindest indulgence which you have shown me all through my life. – & you may rely upon it I will never mention the subject again. …
Believe me my dear Father
Your affectionate son, Charles Darwin. "

Charles Darwin to
Robert Waring Darwin,
31 August 1831

Robert Waring Darwin

Josiah Wedgwood II

(1) It is reputable to my character as a Clergyman here after

(2) A wild scheme

(3) That they must have offered to many others before me. the place of Naturalist

(4) And from its not being accepted there must be some serious objection to the vessel or expedition

(5) That I should never settle down to a steady life here after

(6) That my accomodations would be. most uncomfortable

(7) That you should consider it as again changing my profession

(8) That it would be a useless undertaking

" 1. I should not think that it would be in any degree disreputable to his character as a clergyman. I should on the contrary think the offer honorable to him, and the pursuit of Natural History, though certainly not professional, is very suitable to a Clergyman …
8. The undertaking would be useless as regards his profession, but looking upon him as a man of enlarged curiosity, it affords him such an opportunity of seeing men and things as happens to few. You will bear in mind that I have had very little time for consideration & that you & Charles are the persons who must decide.
I am, My dear Doctor, Affectionately yours, Josiah Wedgwood "

Josiah Wedgwood II to
Robert Waring Darwin,
31 August 1831

HMS Beagle

SIMON KEYNES

HMS *Beagle* may not have won any battles, or broken any records, but she deserves to be remembered alongside HMS *Victory*, and the *Cutty Sark*, as a symbol of achievement in a great age of exploration and discovery. The fact that Darwin was able to make such effective use of the opportunity, and that his observations led directly to the formulation of his theory of evolution by natural selection, is just part of the reason. In her first two voyages (1826–30 and 1831–6), the officers and men of the *Beagle* contributed significantly to knowledge of the coastal regions of one continent (South America), and then to the determination of longitudes around the

This detailed scale model of HMS Beagle was commissioned by Simon Keynes, one of Darwin's great great grandsons, following research into the alterations FitzRoy made to the vessel. Some idea of the extremely cramped conditions on board is given by the figures of Darwin and FitzRoy standing on the deck.

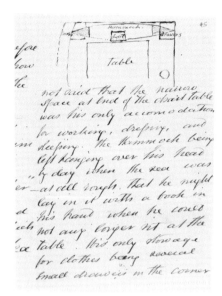

Sketch showing the position of Darwin's hammock in the Beagle's poop cabin, drawn by B.J. Sulivan, Lieutenant on the Beagle, in a letter to Francis Darwin.

Darwin's pencil annotations on a plan of the Beagle's poop cabin, showing the map table and all-important bookcases.

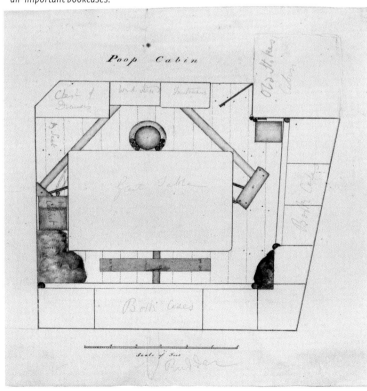

globe; and they went on in her third voyage (1837–43) to chart the coast of another continent (Australia). This was no small achievement for a Ten Gun Brig.

The *Beagle* was built at Woolwich dockyard, on the Thames, in 1819–20. She was about 90ft (27.4m) long on her main deck, and 24ft 6in (7.5m) wide at her widest point. For five years she remained in dock at Woolwich. In 1825 the *Beagle* was modified for surveying work by the addition of a poop deck over the rear part of the quarter deck (abaft the main mast), creating a poop cabin underneath; at the same time she was converted from a two-masted brig into a three-masted barque, with a mizzen mast (carrying a fore-and-aft sail) added behind the main mast, for greater manoeuvrability. On resuming command of the *Beagle* in 1831 for her second surveying voyage, FitzRoy made some further modifications in the light of experience gained in his first captaincy in 1828–30. She would carry two 28ft whaleboats, in addition to five other ship's boats, to aid the work inshore; she would be equipped with more than twenty marine chronometers, for measuring time at certain places around the globe in relation to time at Greenwich, and thereby establishing their longitude; and she would be made more seaworthy.

Knowledge of the *Beagle's* upper deck and interior layout is dependent in large part on a series of sketches made from 'old drawings and recollections' in 1891 by Philip Gidley King, a midshipman on the first and second surveying voyages. The layout of the poop cabin, below the poop deck, is known additionally from a scale drawing prepared probably in 1831, annotated at a later date by Darwin himself. It was here that Darwin worked, seated with his microscope at the chart table and surrounded by useful cupboards; and it was here, over the left side of the table, that he would sling his hammock whenever he needed to 'take the horizontal' in order to alleviate his seasickness or to get some sleep. John Lort Stokes, Mate and Assistant Surveyor, had a small berth adjacent to the poop cabin. On the quarter-deck, underneath the break (or overhang) of the poop deck, was the ship's wheel, from which point one looked forward over skylights for the captain's cabin and the gunroom, towards the main mast and foremast beyond; but the dominant feature when the ship was at sea must have been the two large whaleboats, stowed upsidedown over this part of the quarter-deck. Further forward on the upper deck, between the main mast and the foremast, was the ship's yawl, with the cutter nesting inside it. Immediately in front of the foremast was the forecastle, where Darwin was able to store more of his specimens. On the *lower* deck, the captain's cabin, forward of the mizzen mast, with a sentry at the door, contained FitzRoy's writing-desk and bed, and also the table where FitzRoy and Darwin would sit for dinner. Beyond that were the gunroom (for the junior officers and others) and the midshipmen's berth; Lts Wickham and Sulivan, as well as the Master, the Surgeon, the Purser, and some others, had their own small berths to either side. Forward of the main mast was the main accommodation for the sailors and marines, with mess tables and chests, and steps leading to the upper deck through the main and fore hatchways. Bread, beef, pork, water and other essential supplies were stored below the lower deck in barrels, casks and other receptacles.

Following her return from Australia in 1843 after her third surveying voyage, the *Beagle* became a coastguard watch vessel, and from the late 1840s was based at Paglesham, on the river Roach, in Essex. In May 1870 she was sold by the Admiralty for £540, and is presumed to have been broken up for scrap. Very little survives of the ship herself, though it is possible that the lower part of her hull may yet remain buried in the mud where she lay in the last years of her service.

> *Never did I think so highly of our present Government, as when I heard they had selected Charles Darwin for Gt. Naturalist & that he was to be trans-ported (with pleasure of course) for 3 years – Woe unto ye Beetles of South America, woe unto all tropical butterflies.*
>
> From Frederick Watkins [18 September 1831]

Robert FitzRoy (1805–65)

SIMON KEYNES

Command of the Beagle

In 1828 HMS *Beagle*, under the command of Captain Pringle Stokes, was charting the coast of the southern part of South America. Towards the middle of June, the *Beagle* ran into the worst weather that Stokes had ever encountered, and took refuge in Port Otway, on the south-west coast of Patagonia, in order to make repairs. When the surveying work resumed, the captain fell into such a state that he shut himself up in his cabin. The *Beagle* made her way back south into the Strait of Magellan, arriving at Port Famine on 27 July. A few days later Captain Stokes shot himself.

The naval officer selected by Admiral Sir Robert Otway, commander-in-chief of the South American station, to take over command of HMS *Beagle* was his own flag-lieutenant, Robert FitzRoy. From Rio de Janeiro, FitzRoy took the *Beagle* back south into the Strait of Magellan, out into the Pacific, and then up the west coast to San Carlos on the island of Chiloé; from here he was to sail south into the waters of Tierra del Fuego, to search for passage that would enable small vessels to cross from the Atlantic into the Pacific without doubling the Horn. In mid-April 1830 FitzRoy discovered the 'Beagle Channel', and by the beginning of August the *Beagle* was back at Rio.

Second surveying voyage

FitzRoy's command of the *Beagle* in 1828 to 1830 forms an essential part of the background to the *Beagle*'s second surveying voyage, in 1831–6. After failing to win a parliamentary seat in the election of March 1831, FitzRoy decided to resume his naval career. He was soon given the opportunity to return to South America in

Vice-Admiral Robert FitzRoy, based on a photograph taken of him (in civilian clothes) shortly before his death in 1865. The painting was commissioned by the surviving officers of the Beagle in 1882, for presentation to the Royal Naval College, Greenwich.   SK

the *Beagle*, not only to continue the survey of the south-eastern and south-western coasts, but also to establish a more accurate chain of meridian measurements around the globe for the effective determination of longitude. Yet there was more to it even than that. When first in Tierra del Fuego, FitzRoy had conceived a notion to improve the lot of the native Fuegians, and had brought four of them back with him to England with a view to teaching them the rudiments of the English language, and introducing them to English customs, before returning them to their own land. Frustrated by lack of onboard scientific expertise, and concerned about the loneliness of command, he had resolved that were he ever to return to those parts he would take with him 'a gentleman companion, a person qualified to examine the land', while he and the officers would 'attend to hydrography'. After due consultation the choice fell on the young Charles Darwin.

FitzRoy's experience of the voyage is given in his published narrative, supplemented by his official and private correspondence with the Hydrographer, Francis Beaufort, and by a series of letters written from the *Beagle* to his sister Fanny. FitzRoy comes across as a man with much on his mind, possessed of a quick temper, and prone, under duress, to fits of depression. He is known to have argued with Darwin about slavery, and perhaps also about politics, but it is clear that they enjoyed animated discussion of many other subjects. Most importantly, FitzRoy emerges as an exemplary seaman, who commanded the admiration and respect of his officers and men.

Conrad Martens's sketch of Beagle and Adventure at anchor off the island of Chiloé, 2 July 1834.

Point Arenas

Later career

Following the *Beagle*'s return to England in early October 1836, FitzRoy focussed his attention on the completion of his charts, and on the production of the three-volume *Narrative* (1839), covering the *Beagle*'s first and second voyages. After a difficult spell as the second Governor of New Zealand (1843–5), he was appointed Superintendent of Woolwich dockyard (1848–9), and then, following retirement from the navy, Superintendent of the Meteorological Department of the Board of Trade. Here he made significant contributions to the development of weather forecasting and storm warning.

Fitzroy remained in contact with Darwin, visiting Down House on at least two occasions, in 1856 and 1857. It is clear, however, that he was deeply aggrieved by the publication in 1859 of *On the Origin of Species*, and at the British Association meeting in June 1860 was seen waving a bible above his head in protest at the views of his former shipmate.

On 30 April 1865, in a state of depression induced by various troubles and disappointments, FitzRoy took his own life. His achievements are symbolised by the admiralty charts published as a result of the *Beagle*'s surveying work, and by the barometers which bear his name. More recently, his role in the development of the Meteorological Office has been commemorated by the designation of a sea area off north-west Spain as 'FitzRoy'; and so it is that one can hear his name every day in the shipping forecasts on the radio.

66 *The Beagle now looks something like a ship . . . I get into a fine naval fervour whenever I look at her. I suppose she is as good a ship as art can make her – and if I believe all I hear the Captain is as perfect as nature can make him – It is ridiculous to see how popular he is, ladies can hardly splutter out big enough words to express their big feelings* 99
Darwin to his sister Caroline, 12 November 1831

'I am so surrounded with troubles and difficulties of every kind ...'. Letter from Captain FitzRoy to his sister, Fanny, 6 November 1834. FitzRoy had come close to resigning his commission in a fit of depression.

Cambridge University Library: The Darwin Archive

ALISON M. PEARN

The Darwin Archive in Cambridge University Library, with its hundreds of manuscripts and thousands of letters, is the documentary record of Darwin's entire working life.

The Cambridge Darwin Archive has had adventures of its own. Parcelled up and kept in trunks and cardboard boxes, dispersed, mislaid, rediscovered, and narrowly avoiding incineration, this collection of letters, manuscripts, books, and copies of Darwin's own publications, provides a unique and remarkably comprehensive window into Darwin's life and mind.

Francis Darwin, Darwin's third son, later lecturer in botany at Cambridge, had collaborated in Darwin's botanical research and inherited most of his father's papers; he was the first of several descendants to write about Darwin's life, publishing two edited selections of letters. When Francis died in 1925, the core of the collection was packed up into five metal deed boxes and passed to his son Bernard, who in 1932 compiled the earliest extant catalogue. Ten years later, the family returned some items to Darwin's former home of Down House in Kent (by then a memorial museum), but decided that the bulk should go to Cambridge University Library as a research archive. Nothing was done until after the war however, and when the collection was finally moved in 1948, one entire box and quite a number of individual items could not be found. The missing 'Black Box' as it came to be called, turned up some years later and was then put into store, only arriving in Cambridge in 1962. By then some of the original contents had disappeared, but, tossed into it over the years as they had

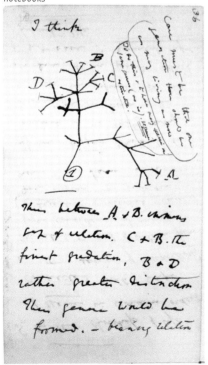

'Thus genera would have formed': Darwin's famous diagram of branching genera and species – the 'tree of life' – from one of his 'transmutation notebooks'

Darwin's experiment book in which he kept notes of botanical experiments conducted in his garden and greenhouse from 1855 to 1868

turned up, were many of the papers missing from the other boxes, together with a substantial number of previously uncatalogued family letters, sheafs of Darwin's working notes, and all of his pocket diaries. A year later Darwin's great-grandson, Robin, came across a further fifteen parcels containing more than 4,000 letters to Darwin, which he recognised as part of a batch of papers he had rescued from a bonfire some years before. These were bought by the University Library and added to the archive in 1975.

Since then, acquisitions and further gifts have brought the total manuscript collection to more than 80,000 individual items in nearly 300 boxes and bound volumes, and all the items listed in Bernard Darwin's catalogue have now been reunited. A recent gift by a member of the family was found to contain the last missing piece, a 'Memorandum book' written in the form of letters to an unnamed friend when Darwin was twelve. It is Darwin's earliest known writing.

The *Beagle* records

More than twenty substantial bound volumes of letters and notes written during the voyage are now in the Cambridge Darwin Archive, together with a spectacular series of geological sections, maps, and other documents. These include thirteen volumes of geological notes and observations, and four volumes of zoological observations. The 'Zoology Notes', begun in 1832, are an orderly record of observations and thoughts, illustrated with pencil sketches of specimens observed

This little 'Memorandum book' of letters to an unnamed friend, was written when Darwin was twelve. It contains charming glimpses into his home and school life. He defends his brother against their sisters' complaints that he was 'out of temper', saying 'just the reverse I think Erasmus very good humered'.

A true scientist, the young Darwin tabulated the advantages and disadvantages of marriage. Marriage won, and the home he shared with his wife Emma and their children was the setting within which Darwin did most of his thinking and writing.

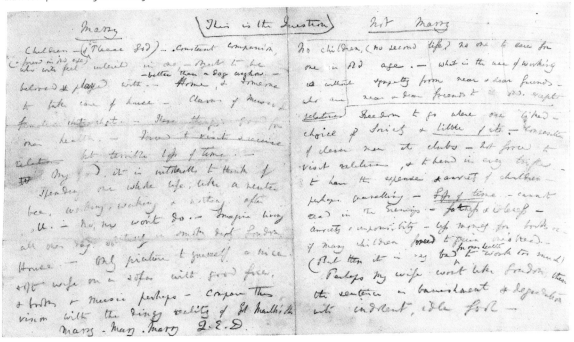

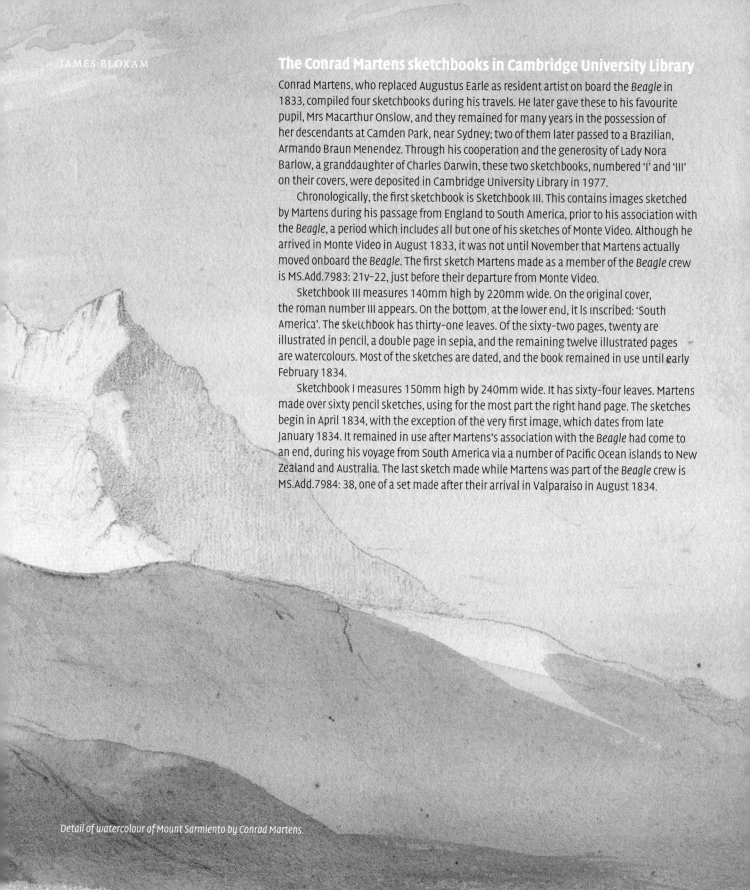

JAMES BLOXAM

The Conrad Martens sketchbooks in Cambridge University Library

Conrad Martens, who replaced Augustus Earle as resident artist on board the *Beagle* in 1833, compiled four sketchbooks during his travels. He later gave these to his favourite pupil, Mrs Macarthur Onslow, and they remained for many years in the possession of her descendants at Camden Park, near Sydney; two of them later passed to a Brazilian, Armando Braun Menendez. Through his cooperation and the generosity of Lady Nora Barlow, a granddaughter of Charles Darwin, these two sketchbooks, numbered 'I' and 'III' on their covers, were deposited in Cambridge University Library in 1977.

Chronologically, the first sketchbook is Sketchbook III. This contains images sketched by Martens during his passage from England to South America, prior to his association with the *Beagle*, a period which includes all but one of his sketches of Monte Video. Although he arrived in Monte Video in August 1833, it was not until November that Martens actually moved onboard the *Beagle*. The first sketch Martens made as a member of the *Beagle* crew is MS.Add.7983: 21v–22, just before their departure from Monte Video.

Sketchbook III measures 140mm high by 220mm wide. On the original cover, the roman number III appears. On the bottom, at the lower end, it is inscribed: 'South America'. The sketchbook has thirty-one leaves. Of the sixty-two pages, twenty are illustrated in pencil, a double page in sepia, and the remaining twelve illustrated pages are watercolours. Most of the sketches are dated, and the book remained in use until early February 1834.

Sketchbook I measures 150mm high by 240mm wide. It has sixty-four leaves. Martens made over sixty pencil sketches, using for the most part the right hand page. The sketches begin in April 1834, with the exception of the very first image, which dates from late January 1834. It remained in use after Martens's association with the *Beagle* had come to an end, during his voyage from South America via a number of Pacific Ocean islands to New Zealand and Australia. The last sketch made while Martens was part of the *Beagle* crew is MS.Add.7984: 38, one of a set made after their arrival in Valparaiso in August 1834.

Detail of watercolour of Mount Sarmiento by Conrad Martens.

under the microscope. It is here, in an undated note on the Galápagos mocking birds (*Mimus thenca*) made sometime in the summer of 1836, that Darwin expressed his first doubts on the immutability of species.

The Cambridge collection of material from this period of Darwin's life has been augmented by a number of significant acquisitions. Among them, two of the sketchbooks owned by the *Beagle*'s artist, Conrad Martens, acquired in 1977, a number of Robert FitzRoy's letters, and a bound collection of his survey maps.

The making of *Origin*

In 1836, in the last months of the *Beagle* voyage, Darwin made the first entries in a small leather-bound pocket notebook. This was the Red Notebook in which Darwin, alongside the *Zoology Notes*, recorded his first known speculations on the transmutation of species. The notebook itself is part of the Down House collection, with a few excised leaves among the papers in Cambridge. Over the next few years Darwin filled seven further notebooks with private, and often cryptic, jottings. Four of these, notebooks B, C, D, and E, now in the Cambridge collection, Darwin referred to as 'Notebooks on the Transmutation of Species', they show the development of Darwin's thinking about species from the initial stirring of doubt about their fixity to the first fully worked out accounts of the mechanism of natural selection. In 1842

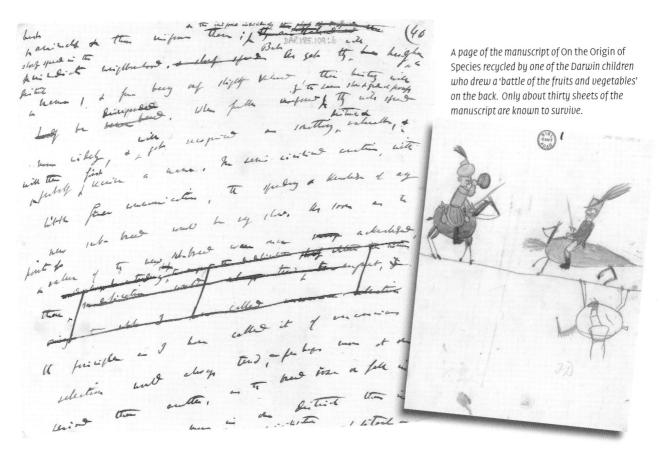

A page of the manuscript of On the Origin of Species *recycled by one of the Darwin children who drew a 'battle of the fruits and vegetables' on the back. Only about thirty sheets of the manuscript are known to survive.*

A page of geological speculations from Darwin's Red Notebook begun in the last months of the voyage.

The recipient of this previously unknown letter bought by Cambridge University Library in 2006, has been identified as John Medows Rodwell, an old friend of Darwin's. The letter was written in October 1860 replying to Rodwell's doubts about the arguments put forward in Origin. Darwin writes 'I am very far from being surprised at anyone not accepting my conclusions on the origin of species', but continues 'I have some confidence that I am in the main right'.

he outlined his arguments in a 35 page manuscript known as the 'Pencil sketch', and in 1844 enlarged that to a 230 page essay. Both these manuscripts are also in the Cambridge archive.

From 1854, once his *Beagle* books and papers were published and his work on the taxonomy of barnacles complete, Darwin began to flesh out the 1844 essay with a mass of data he had been patiently collecting on plants and animals from around the world, and by 1858 had written twelve substantial chapters of a major work he intended to call *Natural Selection*. The arrival of a letter from Alfred Russel Wallace outlining an identical idea, prompted the rapid publication of the much shorter book that we know as *On the Origin of Species*, but the manuscript of the abandoned 'Big Book' is preserved in the Darwin Archive. Of the original manuscript of *Origin* itself, only around thirty sheets survive, nineteen of these in the Cambridge collection. Darwin routinely reused the backs of his manuscripts for notes, or gave them to his children as scrap paper. Of the leaves in the Cambridge collection, many were apparently kept by the family not because of the importance of the manuscript, but for the children's whimsical drawings on the other side.

The letters

For all his working life, Darwin used letters as a way both of discussing ideas and gathering the 'great quantities of facts' that he used in developing and supporting his theories. They form a fascinating collection from many hundreds of correspondents, containing diagrams and drawings, personal observations, photographs, and even specimens. So many letters flowed in that Darwin had a habit of burning batches of old letters when he ran out of space, keeping only those from close friends and family, or those still useful for his research. From the early 1860s however, he tended to keep more of them and, despite later hazards, there are around 8000 in the Darwin Archive. The core of the collection is the several hundred letters exchanged by Darwin and his closest friend, the botanist Joseph Dalton Hooker, and given by Hooker to Francis Darwin after Darwin's death. These letters provide both sides of an extended conversation that took place over more than forty years. Francis, who was editing his father's letters for publication, appealed for other collections; some he was able to keep, but he also made many hundreds of copies of letters that he was only lent, adding these also to his archive. Today the Darwin Correspondence Project research team based in Cambridge University Library continues what Francis started by searching out, transcribing, and publishing complete texts of all known surviving Darwin letters, wherever in the world they are kept.

Darwin's research library

Over the course of his lifetime Darwin amassed a huge collection of books and scientific journals relating to his wide interests. These were given by Francis

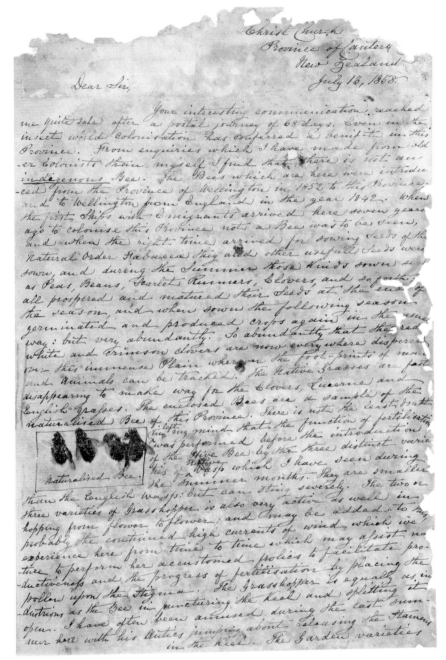

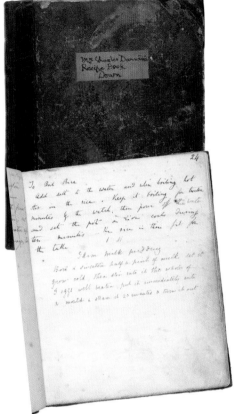

Despite learning to cook while on the Beagle voyage, Darwin wrote only one recipe in his wife's recipe book – 'To Boil Rice'

It wasn't just information that came to Darwin through the post: specimens of naturalised bees sent from New Zealand in 1858, are still stuck to this letter.

Darwin to the Botany School (now the Department of Plant Sciences) in Cambridge in 1905, and deposited at Down House in 1935. Darwin jotted notes in any book that interested him – and even tore them in half if they were unwieldy. In 1960 all the periodicals, and all the books in which Darwin had written, were transferred to Cambridge University Library. Together with his letters, the marginal notes that Darwin made in books and papers are vital to an understanding of the development of his thought, and the genesis of his published writings.

A little reading, thinking and hammering

Plymouth to South America, December 1831 – February 1832

The *Beagle's* first landfall should have been Tenerife in the Canaries, but news of an outbreak of cholera in England had preceded them and rather than wait out the quarantine period FitzRoy decided to press on. Darwin, already suffering from the seasickness that he never overcame, was bitterly disappointed, but between bouts of illness lying in helpless misery in his hammock, he was already at work. He had made good use of his time in London and Plymouth to buy the best scientific equipment he could get. Along with a single-lens Bancks microscope, a clinometer for measuring slopes, a vasculum (a container for botanical specimens), geological hammers, and a quantity of books, he had commissioned a dragnet specially designed to collect surface marine organisms – something that had only been seriously attempted once before.

After three weeks at sea the *Beagle* made landfall at St Jago, a volcanic island in the Cape Verde Islands, and Darwin undertook his first independent geological fieldwork. He energetically collected, tested, and identified rock samples, constructing a cross-section of the island's strata from which he deduced a sequence of eruptions and long cyclical periods of subsidence and uplift. On 15 February they arrived at the remote, barren rocky islets of St Paul's Rocks and Darwin's geological hammer was at work once more.

They were quickly on their way again and on 28 February 1832, a few days after crossing the equator, the *Beagle* lay off the coast of South America.

Some of the surviving books that Darwin had with him on HMS Beagle.

A floating library

For so tiny a vessel, the *Beagle* carried an extraordinary number of books, probably close to three hundred, all of them stored in the 10ft by 11ft poop cabin in which Darwin slept and worked. The library was a potluck of shared volumes, most provided by FitzRoy and related to the official business of the voyage, but many contributed by other members of the crew, and a good number owned by Darwin himself. FitzRoy encouraged him to bring a wide selection and made him a present of several books both before and during the voyage. The 'library' had regulations, and a fixed procedure for signing books in and out – they were a precious commodity.

> " *Fitzroy has an immense stock of instruments & books. – viz takes out 5 Simpisometers, 3 M Barometers. – in books all travels, & many natural history books.* "
> Darwin to J. S. Henslow, 9 September 1831

Among the most significant for Darwin's development as a scientist were the seven volumes of Alexander von Humboldt's *Personal Narrative*, given to him by Henslow, and Charles Lyell's *Principles of Geology*. FitzRoy gave Darwin the first volume of *Principles*, published in 1830, before the voyage; the second reached Darwin in Monte Video in November 1832. Darwin pestered his brother, Erasmus, to keep him supplied with the latest scientific works. The third volume of the *Principles* had found its way to him by July 1834, in time for Darwin to compare Lyell's conclusions about the significance of the Andes in the geographical distribution of plants with his own first-hand observations.

Many of Darwin's *Beagle* books stayed with him for the rest of his life and are in the Darwin Library collection in Cambridge.

Darwin's inscription on the flyleaf of his copy of Leopold von Buch's Travels through Norway and Lapland.

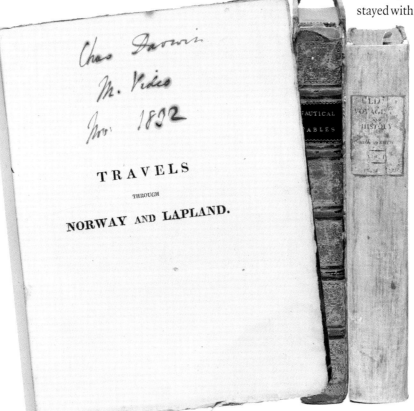

Darwin's observations on the St Paul's Rocks and their modern interpretation

LYALL I. ANDERSON

The crew of HMS *Beagle* spent a single day, 16 February 1832, at the remote rocky reefs of St Paul's Rocks in the mid-Atlantic replenishing food stocks by fishing offshore and killing birds on the island. This was standard maritime practice on long oceanic voyages to provide a source of fresh food and combat scurvy. The detrimental effects of such food gathering on endemic populations of plants and animals were unrecognised at the time and would only occur to Darwin much later on in his life, years after the end of the voyage.

> " St Jago is singularly barren & produces few plants or insects. – so that my hammer was my usual companion, & in its company most delightful hours I spent. "

Even from so short a visit so early on in the voyage, Darwin was able to provide interesting insights into the natural history and geology of this tiny isolated locality.

Being 'entirely destitute of vegetation' the islands provided Darwin with a field geologist's dream: 100% rock exposure! On first approaching the Rocks, Darwin noted that 'they appear from a distance of a brilliantly white colour'. But this appearance was deceptive and he soon discovered that it was down to a covering of bird guano (droppings) rather than any integral physical property of the rocks.

A sample of volcanic scoria collected by Darwin in the Cape Verde Islands, January, 1832

He set to work with his geological hammer and concluded that the island was formed for the most part from what he termed in his notebook 'Serpentine'. This rock is composed entirely of the iron- and aluminium-rich mineral serpentinite, and is relatively 'soft' – it also occurs abundantly in the Lizard Peninsula in Cornwall, and is a familiar sight, carved and polished, in tourist shops.

Serpentinite forms as the result of a chemical reaction between certain types of igneous rocks and seawater. The parent rocks are formed at high temperatures and pressures deep within the Earth's crust. Where cracks and fissures open up in the seabed, seawater is able to penetrate and the alteration to serpentinite begins. Reviewing his notes a little while later Darwin added a footnote to his notebook entry for St Paul's Rocks, summarising an important conclusion that had occurred to him:

'Is not this the first Island in the Atlantic which has been shown not to be of Volcanic origin?'

Although volcanic rocks are a subset of igneous rocks, formed by cooling and crystallisation from a molten state, they have by definition been erupted out of the Earth's crust, rather than cooling at depth below ground. Darwin was therefore correct in stating that St Paul's Rocks are not technically composed of volcanic rock and this obviously presented a puzzle to him. At the time, he had no suitable conceptual framework into which to fit these observations.

It is only with the much later advent of plate tectonic theory and the recognition of the presence of the Mid-Ocean Ridges, the great submarine fractures between

The use and abuse of a geological hammer

It wasn't just rocks that fell victim to Darwin's geological hammer: the birds on St Paul's Rocks, unused to humans, were so tame that the hunter in Darwin could not resist knocking them down like ninepins.

'The first impulse of our invaders of this bird-covered rock was to lay about them like schoolboys; even the geological hammer at last became a missile. "Lend me a hammer?" asked one. "No, no" replied the owner, "you'll break the handle"; but hardly had he said so, when, overcome by the novelty of the scene … away went the hammer with all the force of his own right arm.'
(FitzRoy *Narrative*)

tectonic plates that we can begin to fit Darwin's observations into context. In some respects, the geological setting of St Paul's Rocks is similar to that of Iceland. Both sit relatively high on top of the Atlantic Mid-Ocean Ridge. But whilst Iceland is being pulled apart by plates moving in opposite directions, leading to volcanic eruptions in the fissure between them, movement at St Paul's Rocks is accommodated by faulting and fracturing at right angles to the spreading ridge. Low angle faults provide extension of the crust here, thinning it and uncovering the previously hidden igneous rocks of the sea floor. This faulting regime helps to explain Darwin's observations of the veining and cleavage of the serpentinite. As the Earth's crust below St Paul's Rocks is relatively buoyant due to the hot magma lying at depth, it causes the reefs and islands to break the surface of the ocean and gives us a glimpse of geology normally hidden from view.

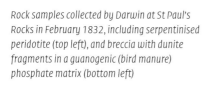

Rock samples collected by Darwin at St Paul's Rocks in February 1832, including serpentinised peridotite (top left), and breccia with dunite fragments in a guanogenic (bird manure) phosphate matrix (bottom left)

Darwin got a lot of advice on what equipment to take with him on the voyage. This oyster trawl was suggested by an Edinburgh University friend, Alexander Coldstream. Darwin had a special net made for collecting marine creatures. Although he could classify only a tiny proportion of what he collected, Darwin saw the importance of the tiny plants and creatures, later known as phyto-plankton and zoo-plankton, to the food chain and started keeping detailed notes of his observations. In his first letter home, anxious to reassure his father that he was making the most of his opportunities, he wrote 'I think – if I can so soon judge – I shall be able to do some original work in Natural History'.

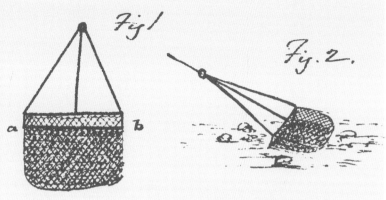

Ship's naturalist?

Darwin's position on board the *Beagle* was never officially that of naturalist; by tradition the ship's surgeon, Robert McCormick, was responsible for collecting and observing on behalf of the admiralty, and he was a rare case of someone with whom the sociable and courteous Charles did not get on. McCormick harboured some understandable professional jealousy for the privileged young amateur, and on Darwin's side was an early contempt for the older man's scientific method. Where Charles had been taught to observe assiduously and amass facts from which to make deductions, he wrote scathingly that at St Jago McCormick did the opposite, making *general* remarks during the first fortnight and collecting *facts* during the last. Darwin was very well aware of the advantages of his independent status

which allowed him to dispose of his specimen collections as he wished. Over the course of the voyage he shipped many dozens of packets and barrels containing thousands of specimens back to Britain, most of them arriving on Henslow's doorstep in Cambridge.

Specimen collecting was a flourishing commercial activity at the time and Darwin joked that there seemed to be more naturalists in South America than carpenters or shoemakers – but he was unusual in collecting not just the physical specimens but also detailed observations of their habits and behaviour, and in the attention he paid to their environment and their interdependence.

Fossil anthozoans collected by Darwin at Bahia Blanca, Argentina, and one of Darwin's pill boxes on which he has written 'Rio Uruguay'. The red label indicates that it contains specimens in the '1000–1999' range, so this is Beagle Catalogue no. 1543 – a box of tiny shells from Rio Negro, Argentina.

ADRIAN FRIDAY

Darwin's Beagle octopus

In his *Beagle Diary*, Darwin records that on 28 January 1832 at St Jago he 'Collected a great number of curious & beautiful animals from the little pools left by the tide.' His *Zoology Notes* also have an entry for 28 January in which he describes his experiences with an octopus in the pools of rocks west of Quail Island, at low water. This specimen is recorded as 'Preserved in spirits No. (50)'. Two days later, on 30 January, he 'Found another.' Then, 'Caught another: I first discovered him by his spouting water into my face when I certainly was 2 feet above him.' An entry for 3 February records observation, but only observation, of a further specimen.

On 18 May 1832, In his first letter to Henslow recounting the voyage so far, Darwin wrote excitedly 'I took several specimens of an Octopus, which possessed a most marvellous power of changing its colours; equalling any chamaelion, & evidently accommodating the changes to the colour of the ground which it passed over. – yellowish green, dark brown & red were the prevailing colours: this fact appears to be new, as far as I can find out.' In his reply, Henslow gently disabused Darwin of that belief: 'I myself caught an Octopus at Weymouth this summer & observed the change of color whenever I opened the tin box in which I put it ... The fact is not new, but any fresh observations will be highly important.'

> *I have so many things to write about, that my head is as full of oddly assorted ideas, as a bottle on the table is with animals.*
> Darwin to Henslow, 18 May 1832

Henslow's gentle correction is reasonable enough. However, it is strange that Darwin himself recorded in his *Zoology Notes* in a paragraph dated 3 February [1832], that Cuvier in his introduction to the Cephalopodous animals 'mentions the fact of changing colour.' His note well precedes his letter to Henslow: had Darwin forgotten – or was he a young man trying a little too hard, at this very early stage in the voyage, to impress his teacher, with the originality of his observations?

The Cambridge University Museum of Zoology has in its collections two specimens of octopus, in alcohol, from St Jago. S. F. Harmer, Superintendent of the Museum of Zoology, who catalogued the specimens in 1901, notes that one was labelled no. 73, and Darwin had written that this was 'same as (50)'. Harmer suggests that 'The second specimen has no label, but is probably the no. 50 alluded to under 73.' The story is more convoluted because a third specimen is listed by Darwin as no. 122, 'St Jago same as (50)' under 'Feb. – March' 1832. So the unlabelled specimen could be either no. 50 or no. 122. Sadly, therefore, we cannot now be sure whether this is the very one that he first observed changing colour so magically.

One of Darwin's octopus specimens, preserved in spirits

I.68248

*Specimens of fish collected by Darwin during the Beagle voyage
and now in the University Museum of Zoology Cambridge*

Not a finished naturalist

Brazil, and Patagonia
February 1832 – November 1832

For the next nine months the *Beagle* covered many hundreds of miles ploughing up and down the coast of Brazil and Argentina checking and rechecking the Admiralty charts. They landed first at Bahia in Brazil (modern Salvador), but a knee injury confined Darwin to the ship and he had to wait for his first experience of tropical forest until they reached Botofogo in April. He was awed: 'wonder, astonishment & sublime devotion fill & elevate the mind'. But the beauty hid danger: a few weeks later three members of the *Beagle*'s crew died suddenly from malaria, the cause of which was then unknown.

His first letters from home had been waiting for Darwin when they stopped briefly at the major naval anchorage of Rio; they had then been away from home for four months. Calling there a second time later in the summer, Darwin got his first real chance to spend time ashore and for two months explored the Corcovado mountains, happily absorbed in collecting specimens, particularly of spiders and wasps.

Then the *Beagle* headed south again, past porpoises and whales, penguins and seals, to Monte Video on the north bank of the wide mouth of the Rio Plata, where they dropped anchor at the end of July. Both Monte Video and Buenos Aires on the south bank, were politically volatile and dangerous places to be – at Buenos Aires the *Beagle* was fired on as a suspected cholera carrier, and in Monte Video the crew helped quell a revolt. For Darwin the flat wide landscape – 'like Cambridgeshire without the trees' – was a disappointment after the lushness of the tropics. By September the *Beagle* was further south still, surveying the coast of Argentina.

On shore again in Patagonia, Darwin was taught how to lasso ostriches by gauchos – the Spanish settlers – enjoyed the company of elegant signoritas, and collected his first fossil vertebrates.

By early November the *Beagle* was back in Buenos Aires to restock for the dangerous voyage down to the Cape.

JOHN PARKER

Handling plants, carrying out instructions

Late in 1832 Henslow received the first box of *Beagle* specimens from Darwin. In response to two letters from Darwin, and having viewed the contents of the box, Henslow wrote back from Cambridge between 15 and 21 January 1833 (although the letter is mistakenly inscribed 1832). In this letter, Henslow offers advice on the information which should be collected along with the geological samples but, in more detail, he describes the qualities necessary for the plant specimens and the methods to be employed in collecting them.

> 66 *For goodness sake what is No. 223 it looks like the remains of an electric explosion, a mere mass of soot – something very curious I daresay.* 99
> From J. S. Henslow, 15 & 21 January 1833 on receiving Darwin's first consignment of specimens

Henslow wrote, 'Avoid collecting scraps. Make the specimens as perfect as you can, root, flowers & leaves and you can't do wrong. In large ferns and leaves fold them back upon themselves on one side of the specimen & they will get into a proper sized paper.' Henslow accompanies this by a sketch of a pinnate leaf indicating 'this side is folded back at the edges.' The sketch bears a striking similarity to a bracken frond from Gamlingay in west Cambridgeshire that Henslow had collected in August 1831 and mounted on one of his herbarium sheets, the lowest pinnae folded back both to fit the sheet and to expose both surfaces with their different morphologies.

Henslow's letter of advice to Darwin about recording his observations and preparing his specimens. Above is Henslow's sketch illustrating how to press and mount large pinnate leaves.

Two of Darwin's surviving herbarium specimens from St Jago, Cape Verde Islands, in Henslow's herbarium are fern fronds of the species *Christella dentata*. These were transported in the first box received by Henslow. One has been inexpertly dried by Darwin to give a tangled mass of pinnae towards its base, the other had to be inelegantly broken by Henslow one third of the way from the apex of the frond in order to fit on the herbarium sheet. It is tempting to think that these two specimens occasioned the instructions about collecting in Henslow's return correspondence.

In October 1835 Darwin collected the fern *Pleopeltis aurea* (now *Phlebodium areolatum*) on James Island in the Galapagos. Two herbarium sheets were prepared by Henslow from this material. The first sheet carries two fronds, both of which indicate that Darwin acted on Henslow's suggestions: the larger frond has the third pinna from the base on its left-hand side folded over, while the smaller frond has both the lowest pinna on the left and the second from the base on the right folded over.

There is a further collection of a highly unusual form of the same fern from October 1835, labelled 'Pleopeltis aurea var.' on the Henslow herbarium sheet. This is a monstrous form of the fern, with four equal-sized and very large pinnae, all originating from a common point rather than the usual pinnate leaf form. Darwin folded over the right hand gigantic 'pinna' for the drying process. He clearly had an eye for monstrous forms in nature, as did his mentor, but he also responded to Henslow's long-distance instructions.

Herbarium sheet with specimens of Phlebodium areolatum *collected and dried by Darwin in October 1835.*

Darwin kept a running list of procedures for handling and preparing all sorts of specimens, and sometimes noted where he got the advice. 'Jars. first half putrid bladder. then 2 coverings of Lead or Tin foil, not large enough to be tied down. then bladder again. then varnish. Garsell'; 'Lap seeds in the Capsule in brown paper, dry but not too hot. Henslow'.

KATHERINE ANTONIW

The Rocks of Rio

Charles Darwin's most far-reaching geological discoveries and theories were chiefly informed by his experiences on the west coast of South America in the second half of the voyage, but by the time the *Beagle* navigated the Straits of Magellan in June 1834 Darwin had already collected in excess of 2000 geological specimens. Discoveries from this part of the journey were often muddied by the young scientist's uncertainty and reliance on the theories of others but his east coast observations had a cumulative impact on the ideas he would later publish.

Whilst the crew of the *Beagle* surveyed the eastern coastline of South America, Darwin explored on dry land, settling for a while at Botofogo Bay, just to the south of Rio de Janeiro, Brazil. Years later, combined with his study of the metamorphic transitions around Cape Town, South Africa, Darwin's geological study of the metamorphic complex of Rio in the summer of 1832, helped him theorise on the origin of metamorphic rocks. The rocks Darwin collected around Rio, mostly varieties of gneiss, now reside in the Beagle Collection in the Sedgwick Museum of Earth Sciences, Cambridge.

Darwin classified gneiss as a 'primitive' rock in his early notebooks, harking back to the tradition of Abraham Werner and his Neptunist scheme of rock classification. According to Werner, gneisses were primary rocks, older and fundamentally different from younger secondary rocks like slate and granite.

Lyell's *Principles of Geology* provided Darwin with new ways of looking at the world and Darwin's observations in Brazil yielded supporting evidence for the unity of origin of these different rock types. By the time Darwin published *Geological Observations on South America* in 1846, he was describing gneisses as 'metamorphic' – literally 'changed shape' – rocks, following the lead of his Cambridge mentors, Adam Sedgwick and John Stevens Henslow.

Silicified wood from the Santa Fe Bajada area, Argentina.

Conrad Martens's sketch of Botofogo Bay, Darwin's first home in South America.

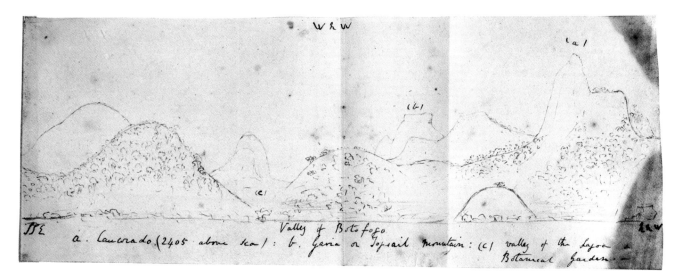

Darwin's own sketch of the terrain near Botofogo, showing relative elevation

Darwin later diverged from Henslow and Lyell in the extent to which he credited massive unseen forces at work within the Earth as the agents of metamorphism. Gneiss has a grain rather like the parallel lines in wood. Sedgwick argued that these lines were formed by the compression of pre-existing ancient bedded sediments. However Darwin interpreted the rocks around Rio as having formed due to igneous intrusion rather than sedimentation. This explained the lines, or folia, as the result of chemical processes during the rock's formation.

Darwin viewed these tiny changes in rock structure as part of the same processes that produced much larger scale features. Observing that all the layers in the gneisses he examined pointed in the same direction led Darwin to build on Alexander von Humboldt's work on aligned geological features across South America, with a dash of inspiration from Darwin's own grandfather, Erasmus Darwin. The younger Darwin posited the existence of electric currents at work deep within the Earth, aligning chemicals as the continents shifted. In an essay on cleavage written in the last months of the *Beagle* voyage, he placed great significance on this alignment, suggesting the grand scale of his observations even in the early stages of the voyage.

This locale also provides us with a rare instance of Darwin neglecting to explain one of his own observations. Darwin noted a large fragment of one type of gneiss embedded in another. Both gneisses exhibited the same foliation and were cross-cut by a granitic dyke. Darwin's assessment of this as 'a unique case' probably reflects either the state of geological knowledge at that time, or more likely a rather ambitious statement from the fledgling geologist.

Darwin's observations from Rio may be messy – his notes from these weeks are notoriously sketchy – but the stories Darwin was later able to publish based on the investigation of this area have something of the grandiose, ambitious and mysterious about them, a fitting result from the first stages of what became so important a scientific voyage.

66 *But Geology carries the day; it is like the pleasure of gambling, speculating on first arriving what the rocks may be; I often mentally cry out 3 to one Tertiary against primitive; but the latter have hitherto won all the bets.* 99
Letter to W. D. Fox from Botofogo, May 1832

Keeping track: Darwin's Beagle records

Right from the beginning of the voyage, whenever he was on shore Darwin kept a small pocket notebook handy to write down rough observations as he made them. Eighteen of these notebooks survive in the collection at Down House. As he collected specimens, Darwin gave each one a unique number, one series for the geological specimens, and two for the organic specimens depending on their method of preservation – whether dried or in 'spirits of wine' – writing labels for the specimens themselves, and keeping running lists of the details including a description, date, and location. His rough field observations were written up as the voyage progressed as separate, fuller, notes on geology and zoology, keyed to particular specimens by number, and Darwin used these extensively in later publications. In the last stages of the voyage Darwin and his servant Syms Covington laboriously copied out his specimen lists, breaking them down into twelve different categories so that they and the specimens themselves could be handed over to the specialists, such as John Henslow, Leonard Jenyns, and Richard Owen, whose task it was to refine the identifications.

Darwin's list of bird specimens in spirits of wine

Darwin used four different coloured labels in succession on his specimens. Specimen '72' (top) with a white label is from Quail Island, Cape Verde. Darwin used white labels first and they denote specimens 1–999. An example of a red label for specimens 1000–1999 is on p. 37. A box of lignite from Chiloé (bottom left) has a green label; Darwin used green for specimens 2000–2999. A fossil gastropod (bottom right) has a very faded yellow label, denoting a specimen in the 3000s – this one is 3852. Darwin wrote the provenance 'Maldonado' directly onto this shell.

Letters from home

'I assure you that no half famished wretch ever swallowed food more eagerly than I do letters.' Darwin to his sister Caroline, 24 October – 24 November 1832

Darwin's three unmarried sisters, Caroline, Susan, and Catherine, wrote devotedly to their brother throughout the voyage, taking it in turns to write a long letter each month giving him all the home news. His brother, Erasmus Alvey Darwin, though happy enough to hunt up the books that Charles asked for, wrote seldom 'not from want of love, but from indolence', and his father, ever the doctor, joked in his one known brief letter that as Charles was 'not a patient' he had nothing to say to him. As he also wrote that he had bought a banana tree just so he could sit under it and think of Charles in the tropics, it is a safe bet his fondness for his son was deeper than he expressed.

Among the very first letters Charles received was one from Catherine written only a few weeks after his departure with the unlooked for news that Fanny Owen, the object of Darwin's one known romantic entanglement before the voyage, was getting married.

'I hope it won't be a great grief to you, dearest Charley, though I am afraid you little thought how true your prophecy of 'marrying and giving in marriage' would prove.'

It was clearly a blow:

'if Fanny was not perhaps at this time Mrs. Biddulph, I would say poor dear Fanny till I fell to sleep. – I feel much inclined to philosophize but I am at a loss what to think or say; whilst really melting with tenderness I cry my dearest Fanny why I demand, should I distinctly see the sunny flower garden at Maer; on the other hand, but I find that my thought & feelings & sentences are in such a maze, that between crying & laughing I wish you all good night.' (To Caroline Darwin 2–6 April 1832).

A portrait of Darwin's sister Caroline.

One of Catherine Darwin's letters to her brother, addressed simply 'Mr Darwin | H.M.S. Beagle | Monte Video | S. America' and sent at the end of April 1832. Four months into the voyage the family had still heard nothing from Charles: 'You cannot think how we all long and talk about your first letter from Rio; what pleasure it will be to hear that you are well and prosperous'.

Cambridge University Herbarium: the Darwin specimens   JOHN PARKER

A herbarium is a collection of dried, pressed plants preserved in the image of life.

Herbarium specimens can be kept virtually for ever if protected from damage by water, fungi and insects. They are usually fixed to single sheets of heavy paper, and sets of single species are then held in folders for long-term storage. The sheets themselves may be labelled with a great variety of information, such as the scientific name of the specimen, the date and place of its collection, the name of the collector, any particular morphological features not immediately clear from the sheet (such as flower colour), ecological details of the habitat, uses of the plant, and so on. Each herbarium sheet, then, is fundamentally important as a reference point for botanical science but can also be understood as a document which can illuminate branches of the humanities and social sciences too.

In botany, herbaria have been, and continue to be, assembled and used almost exclusively for taxonomic studies, as the source material for describing species and varieties, and thus for systematising the plant kingdom. John Henslow, Professor of Botany, however, was not a taxonomist but a physiologist, and yet he began in 1821 the arduous process of gathering an enormous herbarium of his own, concentrating on the flora of Britain. By the time Darwin joined Henslow's botanical class in the Easter term of 1829, this herbarium consisted of over 10,000 British plants and continued to grow rapidly during the rest of Darwin's Cambridge days. The plants for this herbarium had been gathered together by Henslow himself on his numerous and regular field excursions, by his brother and aunts, by his friends in and around Cambridge, via an extensive network of naturalists across the country, and by a small but expanding band of Cambridge students. What then was the purpose of this remarkable herbarium, if not simply as a systematic collection for imparting a general knowledge of British plants to students or for studying their taxonomy?

Henslow's herbarium was an extraordinary research tool developed for his particular approach to experimental botany. His programme from the time of his appointment as Professor of Botany in 1825 focussed on natural populations of plants. It was directed towards understanding the nature of species by defining their morphological limits based on the patterns of variation that they display in nature. To demonstrate these limits, he organised his dried plant samples by a process he called 'collation'. Henslow's collated herbarium sheets each contain between two and thirty-six plants, arranged carefully across the equator of the paper. Each sheet is meticulously labelled with the species name, the date and place of collection, and the name of the collector (even when it was his own gathering) using numbering so that every plant can be identified with a complete set of data.

Two common collation patterns displaying variation in plant size are particularly obvious and striking. In one, Henslow arranged the plants with the largest in the centre, declining in height outwards in both directions, giving a bell-shaped

A watercolour by Conrad Martens of a Lady's Slipper from Elizabeth Island in the Straits of Magellan. A specimen collected by Darwin during the voyage was the first to be described scientifically, and the plant was named Calceolaria darwinii *after him.*

Specimens of Matthiola sinuata, *collected by Darwin in Barmouth, Wales in August 1831*

appearance; in the other, he placed the largest at one edge, with the rest diminishing regularly in size across the sheet. His herbarium sheets also illustrate variation in non-measurement characters, such as leaf-shape, branching patterns and flower colour. Using his collating method, Henslow drew up his own personal list of all the plant species of Britain, established from their patterns of variation, and this he published as a 'Catalogue of British Plants' in 1829. He intended this booklet to be of particular use to his own students during their time at the University and on their outings, so he indicated the plants found in Cambridgeshire for their particular benefit.

As well as his British herbarium, Henslow also gradually accumulated plants from overseas. His younger brother George sent specimens accumulated during his naval tour to both coasts of South America between 1827 and 1829. Some of the Fellows of Cambridge colleges, such as the Rev. Richard Twopeny, presented him with their plant collections made on long vacation tours around Europe. Few of the herbarium sheets using these plants show Henslow's deliberate collation.

The student who supplied the most plants for the Professor's herbarium was Charles Darwin. His first collection, the oldest Darwin specimens known, consisted of five specimens of the rare British plant *Matthiola sinuata* which he obtained from a population at Barmouth on the mid-Wales coast in August 1831. Following this gentle start, he began serious collecting during the voyage of HMS *Beagle*, with contributions every year between 1832 (182 collections) and 1835 (223, mainly from the Galápagos Islands). Altogether, Darwin presented Henslow with about 2,650 plants from the voyage for his herbarium. These were obtained from the mainland of South America, and from a number of island groups such as the Cape Verde Islands in the Atlantic Ocean, the Galápagos Archipelago in the Pacific, and the Cocos and Keeling Islands in the East Indies.

Darwin's plant collections are remarkably similar to Henslow's. Only 30 per cent consist of single specimens, while the remainder range in number from two plants per population to a remarkable maximum of thirty-four (*Galium aparine*, collected in Patagonia in 1832). Darwin accompanied the collections with precise notes made of the date and place of collection, and occasionally added notes.

When Henslow received Darwin's plants in Cambridge, he collated and mounted them onto about 950 of his own herbarium sheets. These were overprinted with 'Mus Henslow' (Museum of Henslow) at the top left hand corner in standard fashion, and also carry an additional brief printed location on the bottom left such as South America, Patagonia or Galápagos Islands. He also added date of collection, name of collector, and brief notes, of particular islands for example, in his own clear hand. Henslow then began to study this magnificent gift, and his own drawings can be found on some sheets. However, the task of identification exceeded Henslow's taxonomic knowledge, and it later fell to Joseph Hooker at Kew to dissect, draw, describe and finally publish Darwin's *Beagle* plants.

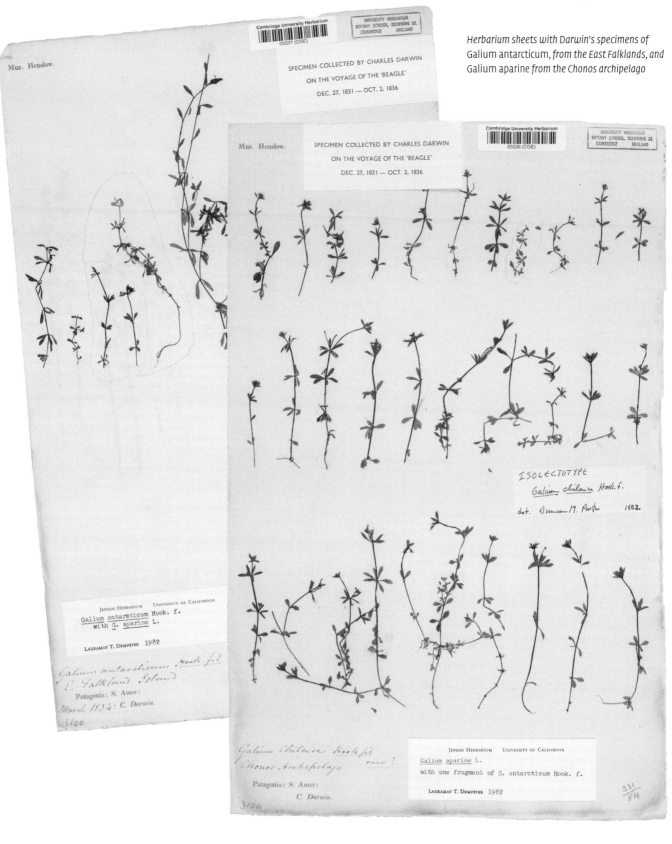

Herbarium sheets with Darwin's specimens of
Galium antarcticum, *from the East Falklands, and*
Galium aparine *from the Chonos archipelago*

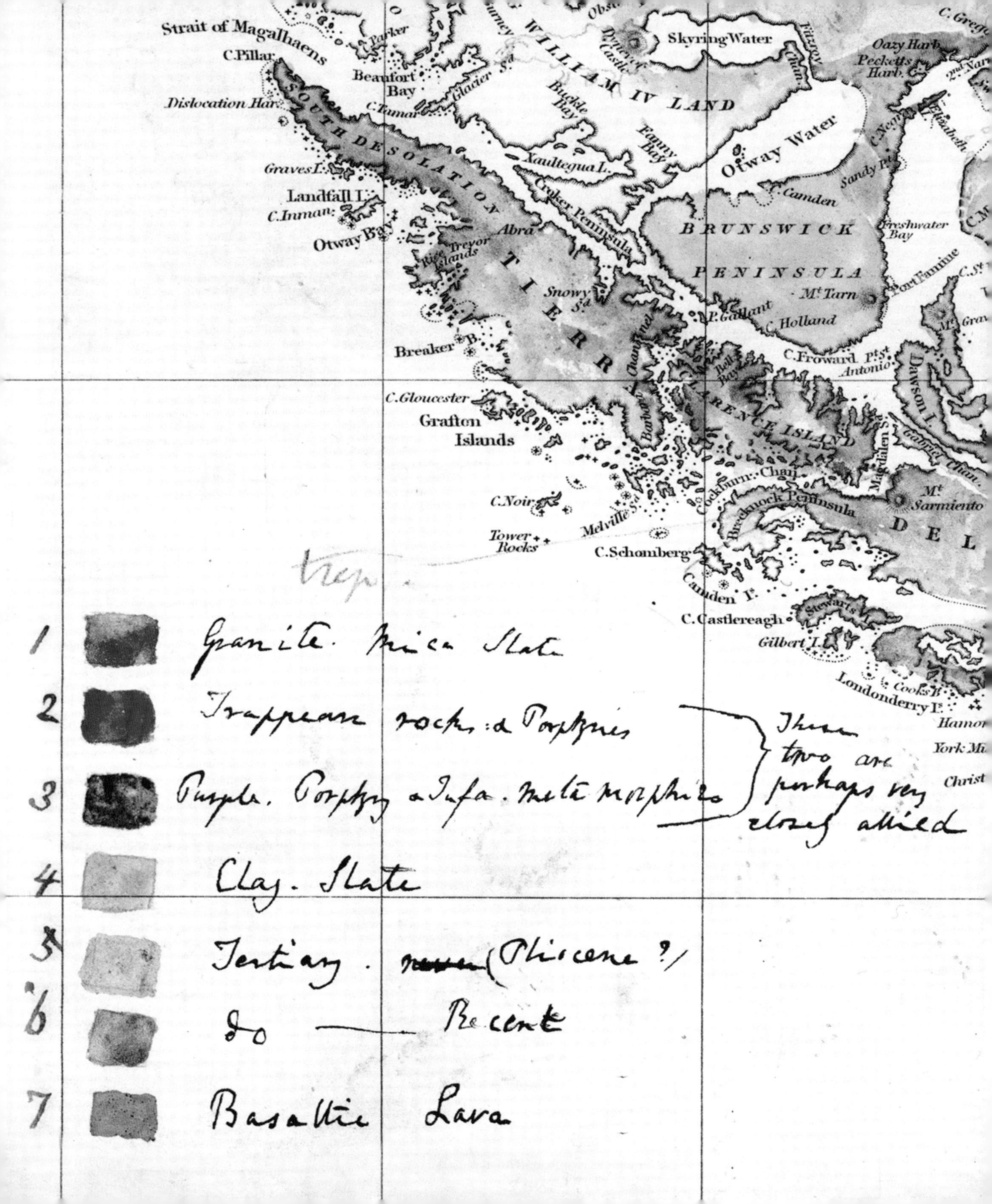

Strait of Magalhaens
C. Pillar
Beaufort Bay
Dislocation Har.
C. Tamar
Graves I.
Landfall I.
C. Innan.
Otway Bay
SOUTH DESOLATION
Parker
Glacier S.
Buckle Bay
WILLIAM IV LAND
Skyring Water
Obs
Furzoy
Castle
Fanny Bay
Otway Water
Oazy Harb.
Pecketts Harb.
C. Gregory
C. Negro
C. Elizabeth
Xaultegua I.
Croker Peninsula
Abra
Trevor Islands
TIERRA
Snowy Sd.
C. Camden
BRUNSWICK
PENINSULA
Freshwater Bay
Mt Tarn
Sandy pt
Port Famine
C. St
Mt Grav
Breaker B.
P. Gallant
C. Holland
C. Froward
Antonio
Pt st
Bell
Bay
CLARENCE ISLAND
Dawson I.
Mt Sarmiento
DEL
C. Gloucester
Grafton Islands
C. Noir
Tower Rocks
Melville Sd.
C. Schomberg
Barbara
Channel
Cockburn Chan.
Brecknock Peninsula
Magdalen Sd.
Gabriel Chan.
Camden I.
C. Castlereagh
Gilbert I.
Stewart's I.
Cooks B.
Londonderry I.
Hanor
York Mi
Christ

trap.

1 Granite. Mica Slate

2 Trappean rocks & Porphyries

3 Purple. Porphyry & Tufa. Metamorphic

} These two are perhaps very closely allied

4 Clay. Slate

5 Tertiary. ~~recent~~ (Pliocene?)

"6 do ———— Recent

7 Basaltic Lava

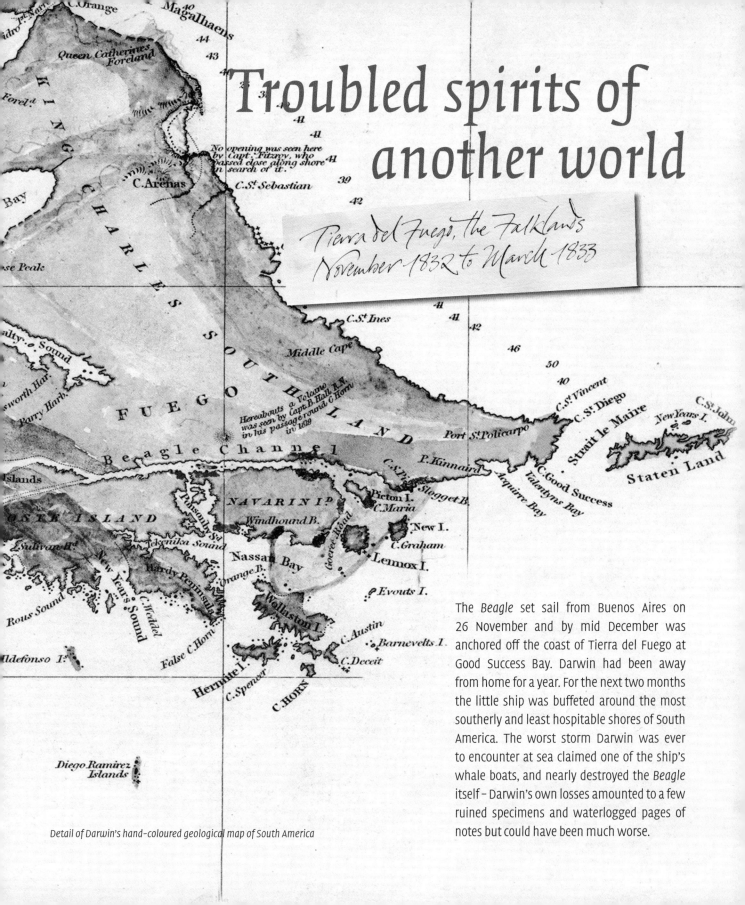

Troubled spirits of another world

Tierra del Fuego, the Falklands November 1832 to March 1833

Detail of Darwin's hand-coloured geological map of South America

The *Beagle* set sail from Buenos Aires on 26 November and by mid December was anchored off the coast of Tierra del Fuego at Good Success Bay. Darwin had been away from home for a year. For the next two months the little ship was buffeted around the most southerly and least hospitable shores of South America. The worst storm Darwin was ever to encounter at sea claimed one of the ship's whale boats, and nearly destroyed the *Beagle* itself – Darwin's own losses amounted to a few ruined specimens and waterlogged pages of notes but could have been much worse.

Tierra del Fuego

FitzRoy had a secondary motive for this part of the voyage. Besides fulfilling his admiralty duties by charting the complex maze of channels woven around the Cape, he was dropping off passengers, repatriating three of the native Fuegians he had taken to Britain on a previous voyage, and leaving with them an Anglican missionary. For Darwin this was his first encounter with native peoples.

Inland exploration here was made almost impossible by the densely tangled Antarctic beech forest clinging to the steep terrain at the coast, but Darwin persevered and made long climbs up to the alpine meadows. Christmas was spent on Hermit Island just west of Cape Horn but conditions were too bad to go on and they retreated to Ponsonby Sound where they set up the mission station and set out in whale boats to explore an arm of the Beagle Channel, a round trip that covered three hundred miles. One night when they were camped on shore near a glacier, a great sheet of ice broke away and crashed into the water sending a wave speeding towards their beached boats. Darwin was among those who reached the boats just in time to save them, and FitzRoy named Darwin Sound after him in commemoration. Returning to the mission station, they found it plundered and FitzRoy reluctantly decided to take the missionary back to the *Beagle* with them.

Admiralty orders were next to survey potential safe havens in the Falkland Islands. They set sail from Tierra del Fuego on 26 February 1833 and arrived at the bleak and windswept islands on 1 March. Darwin had a lot of time to himself there and, although unimpressed with the peaty terrain, made extensive geological observations and was excited by the discovery of fossil shells in 'the very oldest rocks'. Meanwhile FitzRoy, anxious that the *Beagle* alone could not complete their assignments, had impulsively bought out of his own pocket a schooner, which he renamed *Adventure*, and in the early days of April both the *Beagle* and *Adventure* sailed back to the coast of South America.

Tachyeres brachypterus (Tachyeres patachonicus) *the loggerheaded or steamer duck (see p. 90). This specimen was collected by Darwin in Tierra del Fuego and is now in the University Museum of Zoology Cambridge.* 'The steamer is able to dive only to a very short distance. It feeds entirely on shell-fish from the kelp and tidal rocks; hence the beak and head, for the purpose of breaking them, are surprisingly heavy and strong: the head is so strong that I have scarcely been able to fracture it with my geological hammer' (Darwin, Journal of Researches)

Troubled spirits of another world

PAUL WHITE

For Darwin, one of the most dramatic episodes of the *Beagle* voyage was his encounter with the Yahgan peoples of Tierra del Fuego, or the 'Fuegians' as they were called by the English. In a portrait verging on gothic fiction, Darwin described the inhabitants of this 'savage land', their arms thrown violently about their heads, their long hair tangled and streaming, their loud discordant cries, like 'devils which come on the stage in such plays as *Der Freischutz*'. It was with a mixture of curiosity and revulsion, that he recounted his experience in correspondence to family and friends several months later. As he wrote to his sister Caroline, 'I feel quite a disgust at the very sound of the voices of these miserable savages', and yet 'an untamed savage is I really think one of the most extraordinary spectacles in the world'.

Before arriving in Tierra del Fuego Darwin had already observed locals in Cape de Verde, slaves on the coffee plantations in Brazil, and the notorious gauchos of the pampas, but the Fuegians were the first peoples mentioned in Darwin's letters home. All of these would later appear in his published *Narrative*, along with the natives of Chiloé, the Tahitians, and the aboriginals of Australia and New Zealand. But in the Fuegians, Darwin thought he had witnessed man in his most 'primitive wildness'. They represented both the yawning gap between wild and domesticated humans, and the unsettling proximity of the savage and the civilised. The *Beagle* carried three Yahgans who had been taken from their homeland by FitzRoy several years earlier as part of a missionary enterprise, and who were now bound

FitzRoy's letter to his sister, Fanny, of 4 April 1834. He describes an encounter with native Patagonians – 'taller and stouter than any other set of human beings . . . but not giants'; tells her that Charles Darwin is a 'sensible, shrewd, and sterling good fellow'; and recounts the fortunate arrival of Mr Martens to take the place of the artist Mr Earle who had been forced to leave the Beagle at Monte Video owing to 'extreme ill health'

Native Patagonians sketched by Conrad Martens, January 1834

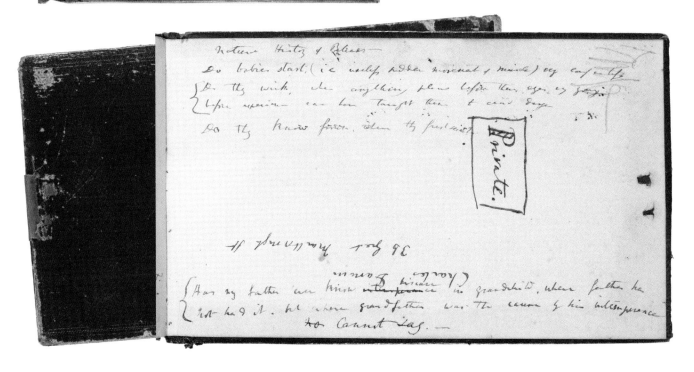

for return. 'Jemmy Button' (Orundellico), 'York Minster' (Elleparu), and 'Fuegia Basket' (Yokcushlu) do not appear in Darwin's letters or *Narrative* until after he has introduced their wild kinsmen, in all their degradation and squalor. It is only at this point that Darwin is struck by the 'progress' that has been achieved through their forced migration to England: 'in contradiction of what has often been stated, three years has been sufficient to change savages, into, as far as habits go, complete & voluntary Europeans'.

Darwin's explanation both for the civilising of the three Fuegians and for the primitive state of their countrymen, was environmental: the harsh and desolate conditions of the southernmost tip of the Americas stunted the higher faculties of human nature. 'How little can the higher powers of the mind come into play: what is there for imagination to paint, for reason to compare, for judgement to decide

From the birth of his first son, William Erasmus, in 1839, Darwin kept a notebook of observations on his children's behaviour and expressions (left).

One of a series of small notebooks that Darwin filled with notes and speculations in the late 1830s and 1840s; this one on 'Expression' is marked 'Private' inside the cover.

As part of his later work on human development, Darwin built up a collection of photographs. This one of Ruth Lockwood, a patient at the West Riding Lunatic Asylum, was one of many sent to Darwin by James Crichton-Browne, the Asylum superintendent

66 No drawing or description will at all explain the extreme interest which is created by the first sight of savages. – It is an interest which almost repays one for a cruize in these latitudes; & this I assure you is saying a good deal. 99
To Caroline Darwin 30 March – 12 April 1833

upon ... Nature, by making habit omnipotent, has fitted the Fuegian to the climate & productions of his country'. Here Darwin was following the prevailing view of naturalists in a long tradition of writing on human 'races'. Climate, diet, and other conditions of existence determined not only the behaviour, but the physical and moral constitution of peoples. Radical modifications of nature, whether in the form of improvement or degeneration, might be effected through alterations in environment. The same theories of acclimatisation were applied to plants and animals in the European colonies.

Although it was not uncommon in this period for native peoples to be collected abroad and exhibited in England and other European countries, both for scientific and theatrical purposes, the *Beagle* did not return with human 'specimens'. Instead, the appearance, customs, and habits of the peoples whom Darwin encountered were recorded in drawings, notebooks, and letters. A number of striking illustrations of Yahgan people appear in the sketchbooks of Conrad Martens. Darwin's *Beagle* diary and correspondence contain minute observations that he would later use for his published *Narrative*. Some of his experiences in Tierra del Fuego colour the pages of his 'transmutation notebooks', begun in the last weeks of the voyage, where he speculated on human ancestry, and the origins of moral behaviour and religious temperament.

Like so many of his experiences during the *Beagle* voyage, Darwin's encounters with the Fuegians remained with him, and formed the basis of ongoing investigations which broadened in scope as he developed his theory of descent. In *Origin of Species*, Darwin was conspicuously reticent on the question of human descent, but he continued to gather information on different peoples of the world. He returned to the subject systematically around 1867, using his global correspondence network, and composing a questionnaire on the expression of emotions to be circulated to missionaries, travellers, and colonial officials. He extended his researches to other human groups (infants, the insane), which he considered especially revealing of the animal origins of human behaviour and expression. To further his researches, he collected photographs from a variety of sources, including studio portraits of children, images of asylum patients, and an album of plates from the laboratory of the French galvanist Guillaume Benjamin Duchenne. Another major source of information was a notebook of observations on his own children, begun on the birth of his first child in 1839, and continued for subsequent children until the early 1850s. When Darwin returned to the Fuegians in *Descent of Man* (1871) and the *Expression of the Emotions* (1872), he was now far from the world of romantic travel and adventure that marked his earlier writing. The people who had once seemed so alien, so far removed from human civilisation, were now reinserted in an argument for the unity of the human species and its common roots in the animal world.

A certain hunter of beetles and pounder of rocks

East Coast inland expeditions - Uruguay, Argentina, Tierra del Fuego and the Falklands revisited, April 1833 - May 1834

The Beagle off the coast of Tierra del Fuego, with Mt Sarmiento in the distance; watercolour by Conrad Martens

By April 1834 the *Beagle* had returned to the familiar country around Monte Video and for the next two months Darwin was able to mount his first long inland expedition and to add larger specimens of birds, animals, and reptiles to his collections. His ambitions had outgrown what he could do alone, and, with an apology to his father who would bear the cost, Darwin hired one of the ship's crew, Syms Covington, as combined personal servant and research assistant. The *Beagle* sailed south again to the Rio Negro in July, and for Darwin and Covington the rest of the year was spent in a series of long cross-country expeditions, rejoining the *Beagle* at intervals as it moved back up the Argentinian coast. It was dangerous, politically unstable, country. Darwin witnessed the brutal and systematic extermination of the native people by the Argentinian settlers, and trod a delicate path through the faction-fighting of the settlers themselves.

By the end of September Darwin was back in Buenos Aires having ridden 400 miles from Bahia Blanca, and in early November was in Monte Video to meet the *Beagle*, and its new artist, Conrad Martens.

Both *Beagle* and *Adventure* sailed south on 6 December and over the next four months reprised the previous year's expedition down the coast of Patagonia to Tierra del Fuego – where they saw the repatriated Fuegian, Jemmy Button – again, and back to the Falklands.

Then, on 13 April 1834, they returned to the mainland, anchoring in the mouth of the Rio Santa Cruz. Some weeks earlier, off Port Desire in Patagonia, the *Beagle* had struck a submerged rock and damaged its copper-clad keel and the time had come to repair it. While the ship was out of action, FitzRoy took the opportunity to lead a major inland expedition. It took three weeks to drag the boats 140 miles upriver, and three days to sail back down. For Darwin, between spells hauling on the long ropes, it was a chance to supplement the geological observations he had made the previous year.

With the *Beagle* repaired they were ready to sail south for a third time, finally rounding the Cape and reaching the west coast of South America in June 1834.

Conrad Martens (1801–1878)

Conrad Martens was born in London, the son of an Austrian diplomat. He studied landscape painting under watercolourist Copley Fielding (1789–1855), who also briefly taught Ruskin. In 1833 he was on board the *Hyacinth*, headed for India, but en route in Rio de Janeiro, learned that FitzRoy was looking for a replacement after Augustus Earle, the *Beagle*'s original artist, had become seriously ill. Martens sailed on the *Indus* to Monte Video where he joined the *Beagle* crew in July 1833; he stayed with them until July 1834, when FitzRoy sold the *Adventure*. In December 1834 Martens headed for Tahiti and Moorea, then New Zealand, and continued to Australia, arriving there in April 1835. In Sydney he was befriended by Philip Parker King, former commander of the British South American Survey, to whom FitzRoy had given him a letter of introduction.

When the *Beagle* arrived in Australia in 1836, Darwin and FitzRoy visited Martens and both commissioned watercolours. In 1837 some of Martens's Australian watercolours were exhibited at the Royal Society of British Artists in London, but he was badly hit by a recession in Australia that lasted through the 1840s and 50s. He turned to oil painting and exhibited at the Victorian Fine Arts Society in Melbourne in 1853, the Paris Universal Exhibition in 1855, and at the International Exhibition in London in 1862, the year in which he also sent Darwin a watercolour of Brisbane River.

Martens stayed in Australia, becoming Assistant Librarian in the Australian Parliamentary Library. He continued painting and had a number of public commissions before dying from a heart attack on 21 August 1878.   JB

Ship's artist

FitzRoy wrote in his *Narrative* of the voyage:

'Knowing well that no one actively engaged in the surveying duties on which [we] were going to be employed, would have time – even if he had the ability – to make much use of the pencil, I engaged an artist ... to go out in a private capacity; though not without the sanction of the Admiralty, who authorized him to be victualled.' Admiralty orders were that drawings used to complement surveys should be 'plain, distinct roughs' rather than highly finished plans, 'where accuracy is often sacrificed to beauty'. Martens's sketches suggest that both he and FitzRoy interpreted this brief more widely, and that he was encouraged to illustrate more extensively the landscape and the people encountered on the voyage.   JB

July 18. 1833.

DAVID NORMAN

South American fossils: Darwin's palaeontology

The collection of geological specimens, together with geological observation and measurement, formed the core of Darwin's work each time he disembarked from the *Beagle*. An important and intellectually stimulating component of his collection, however, was the fossils – with which Darwin was far less well acquainted. His first notable discovery was of large fossil mammal bones at Punta Alta in Patagonia towards the end of his first year aboard the *Beagle*. He wrote in his notes, '[T]he number of fragments of bones of quadrupeds is exceedingly great: – I think I could clearly trace 5 or 6 sorts.'

Large vertebrate fossils from South America were already known through Humboldt's discoveries of teeth from *Mastodon* (an elephant-like proboscidean) and remains of *Megatherium* (a giant ground sloth).

Darwin also collected remains that were recognisably mastodont and megatheroid, but his material indicated a far greater diversity of extinct life. Greater understanding of this diversity awaited specialist work back in Britain; however, even at the time of the voyage, he was clearly aware of the general anatomical similarity between some of his new fossils and the distinctively South American contemporary fauna such as 'edentates' (e.g. sloths and armadillos), rodents (guinea pigs, agoutis and capybaras) and ungulates (llamas and alpacas). For example, Darwin had collected fossilised skulls of edentates and rodents, and patches of tessellated, shield-like bony armour that, though considerably larger in size, resembled the bony plates that covered the bodies of living armadillos. He was also intrigued to discover some fossil horse teeth embedded among these ancient remains.

After Darwin's return to England in 1836, Richard Owen, the renowned British comparative anatomist (later founder of the Natural History Museum and staunch opponent of Darwinism) willingly undertook the description and assignment of these fossils. In a major report on the fossil mammals published in 1840, Owen confirmed the presence of a considerable variety of 'edentates': several ground-sloths (*Megatherium*, *Megalonyx*, *Mylodon*, *Scelidotherium* and *Glossotherium*), and a huge armoured animal (later recognised as *Glyptodon*) related to the armadillo, as well as smaller, more typical armadillos. There was also a form of *Toxodon* (a notoungulate – sometimes referred to as a 'gigantic guinea pig'); Owen's 'camelid' *Macrauchenia* in reality a litoptern (an exclusively South American ungulate, anatomically and evolutionarily convergent upon true camels); *Stegomastodon* (an elephant-like proboscidean); hystricomorph rodents (varieties of cavy typical of South America); and, as suspected by Darwin, most unexpectedly, a true horse (*Equus* sp).

Darwin, and indeed Owen, was strongly impressed by a number of facts linked to these 'dry' taxonomic observations about the fossils: the clear biological relationship between the generally gigantic but *extinct* forms and their modern

> **My dear Philos**
> Trusting that you are not entirely expended, – though half starved, occasionally frozen, and at times half drowned – I wish you joy of your campaign with Gen. Rosas – and I do assure you that whenever the ship pitches (which is very often as you well know) I am extremely vexed to think how much sea practice you are losing; and how unhappy you must feel upon the firm ground. **"**
> From Robert FitzRoy, 24 August 1833

> **" ** I am quite charmed with Geology but like the wise animal between two bundles of hay, I do not know which to like the best, the old crystalline group of rocks or the softer & fossiliferous beds. – When puzzling about stratification &c, I feel inclined to cry a fig for your big oysters & your bigger Megatheriums. – But then when digging out some fine bones, I wonder how any man can tire his arms with hammering granite. **"**
> To J. S. Henslow, March 1834

counterparts; their comparative *uniqueness* inasmuch as they were representatives of a truly South American fauna; and their comparatively recent existence. Darwin had been able to demonstrate that the majority of fossil invertebrates (molluscs) found with these extinct mammal bones were similar to those still living, which argued strongly that the sediments dated from a very recent period in Earth history. There was also the extraordinary insight into the history of the horse: unknown to human civilisations in South America prior to the arrival of the conquistadors, it was now clear that ancestral *Equus* had become *extinct* in South America in the geologically recent past.

Such observations probed the heart of vitriolic debates in Paris between Georges Cuvier (1769–1832) and Étienne Geoffroy Saint-Hilaire (1772–1844). Cuvier was a catastrophist and functionalist, who interpreted similarities in anatomy between species as a product of common adaptation to perform specific tasks, with a creator God sweeping all aside in mass-extinction events and then repopulating the Earth de novo. Geoffroy, a disciple of Jean Baptiste de Lamarck (1744–1829), saw progression in the increasing complexity of life with the passage of time, and continuity in nature. In essence, while Cuvier claimed that the legs of man, mice and lizards were similar in construction simply because they performed the function of walking, Geoffroy, in contrast, recognised homology in the limbs of these animals – their bones being similar because they reflect a common 'blueprint' for all vertebrate animals – and insisted that, despite the evidence of local catastrophes, continuity in structure could be demonstrated over geological time.

Owen presented his first Hunterian lectures at the Royal College of Surgeons in the summer of 1837 and, not surprisingly, included mention of Darwin's *Beagle* specimens. Among these was the enormous, but enigmatic, skull of *Toxodon*, which Owen had considerable difficulty placing within his general understanding of the recognised groups of *Mammalia*. The mystery skull had enlarged incisor teeth followed by a large diastema (gap) and then a row of grinding teeth, the arrangement seen in modern rodents. It was as large as the skull of an adult hippo (a modern pachyderm), and it had large nostrils on the top of its snout, as seen in the skulls of elephants and whales. Clinging to Cuvierian principles of comparative anatomy, Owen concluded that *Toxodon* 'manifests an additional step in the gradation of mammiferous forms leading from the *Rodentia*, through the *Pachydermata* to the *Cetacea* ...' While this *sounds* almost evolutionary in its import, Owen was actually approaching the placement of this mystery animal in the context of a metaphor: a sort of Creator's scaffold, within which the

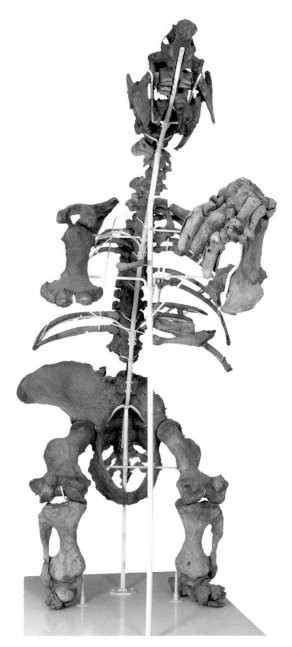

Megatherium, *or giant ground sloth*

" I am become quite a Gaucho, drink my
Mattee & smoke my cigar, & then lie down
& sleep as comfortably with the Heavens for
a Canopy as in a feather bed. – It is such a
fine healthy life, on horse back all day, eating
nothing but meat, & sleeping in a bracing air,
one awakes as fresh as a lark. *"*

To Caroline Darwin, 20 September 1833

diversity of all mammals could be placed. He was in effect treating *Toxodon* like an awkward jigsaw piece that needed placing in a rather complex, but frustratingly incomplete, puzzle.

Keeping his own counsel while the debate swirled around him, Darwin was deeply impressed by the fact of extinction revealed, almost universally, by his South American fossil mammals. He was struck on the one hand by the universality of some extinctions: what could have killed off all the *mastodons* in the northern and southern, as well as the eastern and western hemispheres, simultaneously? And, in sharp contrast, why did the horse become extinct in South America only? Was there a single explanation for such different histories? He was also struck forcibly by the geographic distinctiveness of the South American fauna, both past and present. This became even more important as he began to perceive the South American faunal influence on the Galpágos Islands and the variability and individuality of species between the islands.

Skull of a Toxodon

Darwin's understanding of the fossil record, built through his own field observations and fossil discoveries, as well as by direct exposure to the anatomical expertise of Owen, was crucial to his adoption of 'transmutationism' in March 1837. Against the background of the deeply challenging philosophical and metaphysical struggles in which the discipline of comparative anatomy was embroiled, Darwin was in an ideal position to slipstream the taxonomists and philosophers while developing his own theories.

Fossils of Buccinanops Globulosum. *Darwin wrote 'BA' on them indicating that he found them at Buenos Aires*

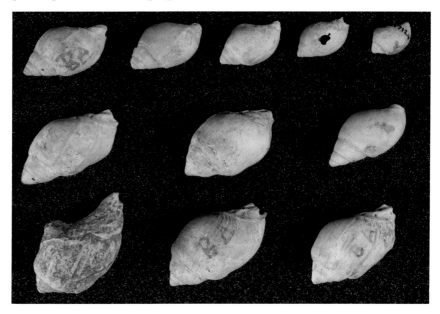

Darwin and Bryozoa

ADRIAN FRIDAY

The colonial animals grouped as bryozoans are poorly known to those who are not zoologists because, although very commonly encountered on the strandline at the seashore, they are often not recognised as animals. The light brown, crisp, dried out bunch of what looks like a seaweed is usually the common bryozoan *Flustra*. It frequently finds its way onto the tops of children's sandcastles. Also very common, but rather less conspicuous, are patches of what appears to be fine, white netting encrusting seaweeds themselves. Each hole in the 'net' is, or was, occupied by an individual 'zoid' of a colony; and each zoid, in its own walling, is connected to other members of the colony. Today, so-called 'modular' animals are of great, interest to evolutionary biologists.

Fossil bryozoa and crinoid stems from the Falkland Islands. Darwin described these as: 'Gorgoniae? In micaceous sandstone organic tissue still present'

Sex and violence are less obtrusive in bryozoans than they are in many other animals, and the group was judged a suitable subject for genteel study by amateurs in earlier decades. Darwin, however, who was hardly a genteel amateur (except occasionally by extreme English self-deprecation), had a long-standing interest in the group. Indeed, when he was attending Edinburgh University in 1826 he read a paper on *Flustra* at the Plinian Society of the University. That early paper was never published.

During the *Beagle* voyage, mostly on its first half, Darwin naturally included bryozoa in his collecting activities. Bryozoan colonies are undemanding to collect, and they are easy to preserve, either in alcohol or as dried specimens, although drying does not, of course, generally preserve the soft tissues. In 1830 the term 'Polyzoa' had been coined for what later became known as 'Bryozoa', although Darwin did not catch up with this name until after the *Beagle* voyage, referring instead to zoophytes or 'corallines'.

The group has had a colourful taxonomic history. As currently recognised, the phylum Bryozoa contains over 4,000 living species, easily enough to keep an expert busy. Most of these are marine, but there is also a minority of freshwater species. Partly because many forms have calcareous walls enclosing the individual zoids, bryozoans tend to fossilise rather well and there are many more fossil species than there are living ones, mostly from the last 150 million years, but from as far back as over 400 million years. Because of the plant-like appearance of many bryozoans, they were once colloquially known as 'moss animalcules', and were included with

Caberea minima

RICHARD DARWIN KEYNES

Well over half the pages in Darwin's *Zoology Notes* are concerned with the small animals and plants to be found in the sea, and in observing their close behavioural adaptation with one another Darwin became one of the founding fathers of ecology. Off the coast of Patagonia at a depth of 10 fathoms in May 1834 Darwin fished up a red-coloured bryozoan, which he at first called *Crisia*, but which was later identified as belonging to the species *Caberea minima*. Darwin observed it carefully under his microscope and drew it in great detail. He noted that it was coated with movable bristles which were controlled by muscular hinges; their function was not obvious, but his experiments showed that they could both appreciate changes in their surroundings and respond by movement of their own. This meant, as he put it, that over the whole animal both 'a co-sensation & a co-will' was operating, a conclusion whose importance he stressed by heavy lining in the margin of the manuscript. For a believer in evolution, the moment when the most primitive creatures first became able to interact usefully with their environment was clearly a crucial one, resulting eventually in the development of all the higher animals. As the manuscript is in ink but the marginal scoring is in blue crayon – a medium Darwin characteristically used in later work – it is likely that the implications came to him only when he reviewed his notes; evolution did not come to him in a flash on that day.

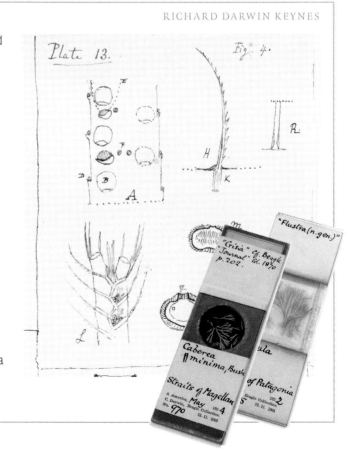

George Busk (1807–1886)

After the *Beagle* voyage, Darwin's collection of bryozoans disappears from the records until the material was sent, in 1852, for study by George Busk, one of the foremost workers on the group of his day. In 1863, on the way down to Malvern Wells, Darwin had cause to consult Busk on quite another matter: a former Hunterian Professor at the Royal College of Surgeons, Busk was asked to prescribe for Darwin's 'stomach symptoms' following a recommendation from Darwin's friend Joseph Hooker, who reportedly described Busk as 'the most fertile brain of any man I know in regard of all such matters as your stomach'. (Busk duly prescribed, but the famous symptoms continued.) George Busk was also on the Council of the Royal Society, and was one of the supporters who persuaded the Society to award Darwin the prestigious Copley Medal, news that was announced in 1864.   A F

coelenterates (animals such as sea anemones, corals and hydra-like forms) in the 'zoophytes'. These names reflect, with impressive etymological accuracy, the early uncertainty over whether bryozoans were plants or animals.

Although Darwin himself had come across at least one species that seemed to be significantly different from the majority, the Polyzoa at this time was regarded as relatively coherent. Later in the 19th century, a group of superficially similar animals known as the entoprocts (and it was one of these that Darwin had recognised as different) was included within the Bryozoa, with the original inhabitants of the phylum being designated the ectoprocts. In the later 20th century, the majority opinion was that the two subgroups of the expanded Bryozoa did not, after all, really belong so closely together. Molecular studies published in 2008 suggest that the ectoproct forms belong in a larger grouping with annelid worms (such as earthworms) and molluscs, and a number of other, less major, phyla; but their precise position remains uncertain. Although entoprocts may also belong in this larger grouping, they are not at all closely related to the ectoprocts. There are only around 150 species of entoproct, and their formal removal leaves the modern Bryozoa equal to the Ectoprocta. Many would prefer that the name Bryozoa disappear, leaving the two distinct groups of Ectoprocta and Entoprocta as phyla.

Characteristically, Darwin's main subsequent interest in Bryozoa was not in their classification, but in their evolution – particularly in features of their anatomy that had fascinated him since his student days in Edinburgh with Robert Grant. These features are the whip-like vibracula and the jaw-like avicularia; particularly, in the case of the latter, in those forms of avicularia that resembled a bird's beak. These details of the bryozoan anatomy feature in letters exchanged between Darwin and George Busk. Essentially, Darwin surmised that the vibracula and the avicularia, though different in appearance might well have been derived 'from the same source' through successive gradations.

Monte Video; Conrad Martens, 28 August 1833

The Sedgwick Museum: Darwin's geological specimens LYALL I. ANDERSON

The *Beagle* specimens now in the Sedgwick Museum were in Darwin's own private collection for many years only appearing in public some time after his death. The Beagle Collection is well-travelled, and not only in the sense that it contains rocks, minerals and fossils from three continents.

The whole collection of geological specimens from Darwin's *Beagle* voyage fieldwork was only gathered together briefly once. This was in Cambridge immediately after Darwin's return. It had been sent back piecemeal during the course of the voyage to John Stevens Henslow on board various ships as opportunity arose. This sensibly insured against wholesale loss through shipwreck, always a risk for the collector whilst engaged in extended explorations far from home, and made space for yet more collected objects in the cramped storage of HMS *Beagle*.

After the voyage, Darwin and Henslow began to carve up the collection and dispatch research material to different specialists. This first dispersal of the collection saw many of the vertebrate fossils sent to London to Richard Owen who subsequently described many of Darwin's fossil vertebrates from South America. These fossils now reside in the Natural History Museum, London. Similar arrangements were made for the fossil invertebrates and palaeobotanical material. In terms of the rocks, Darwin sent some volcanic samples to Charles Daubeny in Oxford: they now form a part of the Oxford University Museum collections. Volcanic rocks from the Ascension Islands and some from the Galápagos now reside with the British Geological Survey's collections, having been donated to its forerunner, the Museum of Practical Geology, by Darwin himself.

What we now recognise as the Beagle Collection held by the Sedgwick Museum suddenly reappears back in Cambridge on Friday 22 January 1897, fifteen years after Darwin's death. George Howard Darwin, Charles Darwin's second son, donated two packing cases of geological samples 'wrapped in canvas bags with numbers attached thereto' to the 'geological museum'. Sedgwick had set up this museum and it incorporated the former Woodwardian Museum along with other collections. In a postcard to Professor McKenny Hughes, now in the University Library Darwin Archive, George Darwin wrote that his younger brother Frank was 'trying to find the corresponding catalogue', probably a reference to Darwin's geological specimen notebooks.

In some ways the gift is not surprising as George Darwin was resident in Cambridge, but the timing suggests that there was a particular motive for this transfer from private to relatively public hands may have had a particular motive. In 1897 the Downing Street site for a proposed new geological museum had just

The Sedgwick Museum of Earth Sciences provides a secure final resting place for the largest single accumulation of Darwin's geological specimens from the period of the Beagle voyage.

Geological samples packed in sauce bottles from HMS Beagle

(Opposite page) A drawer of Beagle specimens from Argentina and Chile as they are stored at the Sedgwick Museum of Earth Sciences. Some of the specimens pictured here are from Darwin's travels in the Andes with Alexander Caldcleugh in 1835.

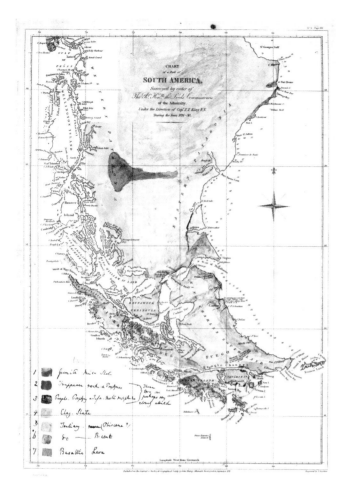

Darwin's hand-coloured and annotated geological map of part of South America, now in the Cambridge University Library Darwin Archive

been successfully purchased and the plans for the museum itself drawn up and submitted. The coincidental donation of this important historic collection may have provided a political lever to advance the case for the establishment of the Sedgwick Memorial Museum, which finally opened in 1904.

So where was this collection during Darwin's lifetime? He only completed his geological studies in 1846 with the publication of '*Geological Observations of South America*' by which time he was already established at Down House in Kent where he lived the remainder of his life. It is probable that the specimens remained with him there almost as sentimental souvenirs of his great adventure. This is important, as it effectively froze the collection in time, together with Darwin's original but already outdated naming scheme for some of the rocks including various 'greenstones'. After Darwin's death in 1882, the rocks and minerals must have been retained within his family, treasured mementos of his life and work. His wife Emma died in October 1896, so perhaps the collection travelled to Cambridge after Down House was given up and its contents cleared.

As usually happens when a geological collection meets museum staff, once in Cambridge George Darwin's gift was apportioned among the curators according to their sectional responsibilities. The lion's share fell to Alfred Harker, a Cambridge graduate who advanced through the ranks of the Geology Department from Demonstrator to Lecturer and finally to Reader in Petrology. Harker eventually published a short note on the Beagle Collection but not until 1907, a full ten years after its arrival. Importantly, he also compiled a handwritten catalogue of the specimens based on Darwin's geological specimen notebooks. His definition of the Beagle Collection was as a petrological rock collection; any fossil content was incidental to the rocks enclosing them. Consequently, although the fossil shells alluded to by Darwin in '*Geological Observations of South America*' were collected during the voyage of the *Beagle*, they are not labelled as belonging to the Beagle Collection: they are stored within the palaeontological collections. Similarly, fossils from the Falkland Islands bear regular Sedgwick Museum numbering rather than the characteristic paper label Harker applied to rocks in the Beagle Collection.

Over 500 prepared microscope sections now accompany what geologists generally term the 'hand specimens' of the Beagle Collection. These sections comprise a slice of rock thin enough to transmit light, mounted on a glass microscope slide. The use of this technique in igneous petrology, which allowed

Pill boxes from the Beagle voyage. The shells inside were packed in cotton wool

refinements to the identifications that Darwin had initially made, was pioneered by Harker. The slide collection itself grew over time as various new techniques for the study of rocks and minerals were developed.

So what does the Beagle Collection actually contain in terms of geological objects? Unsurprisingly the majority of the rock samples are of igneous origin formed from molten magma. There are some metamorphic rocks, changed by heat and pressure below the surface of the Earth. References to sedimentary rocks, formed from the erosion of pre-existing rocks, pepper Darwin's geological notebooks. In terms of economic minerals, there are a suite of metal-bearing ores from the mines of Chile, some coals and lignites and even what we could term a 'china clay' from the Azores. Most samples were collected by Darwin himself, others were collected for him and yet others were gifts from fellow geologists. Each object really does have a story to tell, even if it is only to date more precisely Darwin's overland itineraries.

The Beagle Collection has been variously exhibited and stored in the century since its accession. Aside from a few objects on display within the Department of Earth Sciences, all of the collection is now housed in a purpose-built collections storage facility to the west of Cambridge (the A. G. Brighton Building built in 1991). In July 2009 a permanent exhibition at the Sedgwick Museum titled '*Darwin the Geologist*' will open a new chapter in the history of the Beagle Collection. At last the majority of the collection will emerge from the darkness of storage into the light and the gaze of the general public.

Misery and vexation of spirit

Round Cape Horn; surveying the island of Chiloé, Chile.
June 1834 to December 1834

The rest of the year was a difficult one for the *Beagle*, *Adventure*, and their crews. Most of it was spent surveying around the Island of Chiloé and the Chonos archipelago of southern Chile. Darwin took every chance he could to get ashore, but hated the temperate rain forest where dense tangles of falling trees and rotting vegetation made it hard even to find the ground. There was some respite: moving north, he spent a pleasant stay in Valparaiso and from there explored into the Andes and up to Santiago. But then for two miserable weeks he fell seriously ill, probably with typhoid fever. Meanwhile FitzRoy, who had never got official backing for its purchase, could no longer sustain the cost of the *Adventure* and was forced to sell it; there wasn't enough room on the *Beagle* for both crews and among those who left was the artist Conrad Martens. Worn down and depressed, FitzRoy came close to resigning his commission.

November saw them back once more enduring incessant rain in Chiloé. Darwin found it dull, though among his discoveries, almost unremarked at the time, was a curious barnacle that later played a major role in the development of his evolutionary theories.

Forest scene
at Chiloe

July 9, 188_

SHELLEY INNES

The anomalous 'Mr Arthrobalanus': Darwin's adaptationist approach to taxonomy

In a letter to Henslow in March 1835 Darwin remarked that he had done 'very little' in zoology; the 'only two novelties' he added, almost as an afterthought, were a new mollusc and a 'genus in the family Balanidæ' – a barnacle – which 'has not a true case, but lives in minute cavities in the shells of the Concholepas'. His notebook entry on this aberrant creature, later called *Cryptophialus minutus*, revealed that, in addition to its lack of shell, it possessed only three pairs of cirri – frond-like limbs used for gathering food – instead of six, and, observing its final pre-adult stage, he wondered 'who would recognise a young Balanus in this ill-formed little monster?' Darwin put his specimens away for over a decade, and when he returned to the puzzling little creature in October 1846, he planned only to write a paper on the anomalous 'Mr Arthrobalanus', as it was now known to him. But by the end of November he had asked Richard Owen for further specimens of sessile barnacles with which to compare it, and eventually, Darwin decided to write a complete monograph on both living and fossil Cirripedia. The work took him eight years.

Barnacles are a very odd group of Crustacea. The crustaceans most of us probably know are lobsters and crabs; with an armour-plated body, multiple legs, and large pincer-like claws, a crab scuttling along the sand at low tide is easy to identify. A cluster of acorn barnacles, on the other hand, fixed to a rock and revealed at the same low tide, resembles a miniature volcanic mountain range extruded by the rock itself, and yet these odd creatures are the exo-skeleton in the closet of the crustacean family. Indeed, they remained in the closet until well into the 19th century. They were first placed along with molluscs in the Vermes (testacea) by Linnaeus (1758); Jean-Baptiste Lamarck, recognising some of their internal structural differences, called them 'Cirrhipeda', divided them into sessile and stalked, and made them an intermediate group between sedentary 'Annelides' and 'Conchifera' (1809), but Georges Cuvier, not admitting intermediate classes, soon returned them to his 'Mollusca Cirrhopoda' embranchement (1812).

When Darwin sailed on the *Beagle* at the end of 1831, John Vaughan Thompson's *Zoological researches* (1828–30), was one of the books on board. Thompson was the first to

Darwin's drawings of the barnacle later named Cryptophialus minutus *observed through his microscope on board the* Beagle

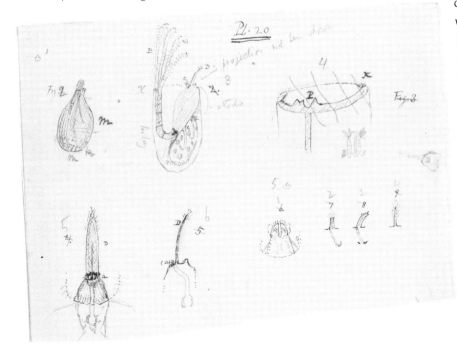

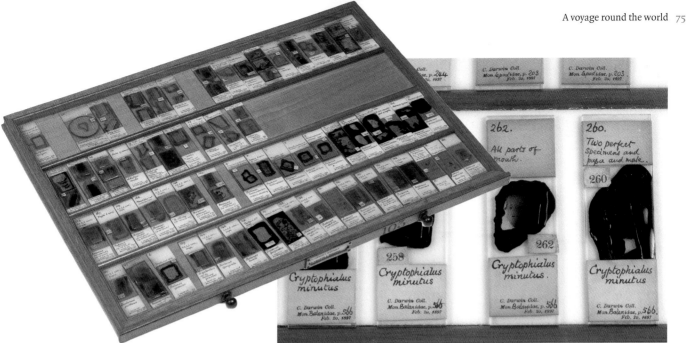

Darwin's microscope slides of barnacles, including several mounted specimens of Cryptophialus minutus

Darwin's passport allowing him to travel in Chile

argue that cirripedes were true Crustacea, based on his observation of a larval stage of *Balanus*. Thompson's view was by no means immediately accepted; the entry on 'Cirripeda' in the *Penny cyclopaedia* of 1837 reads, 'a well-defined natural group of marine invertebrate animals, whose place in the system has occasioned much doubt and difference of opinion among zoologists'.

How and why did Darwin become the person who would dispel much of that doubt and write the definitive taxonomic monograph on the sub-class Cirripedia?

Darwin's interest in marine invertebrates began while he was a student in Edinburgh. Instead of concentrating on his medical studies, he turned his mind to the fascinating world of sea creatures he could observe on the beach at Leith. His first paper, in March 1827, concerned his discovery that the 'ova' of the sea mat, *Flustra*, were ciliated and free-swimming. After recording this observation in his notebook, he added, 'This fact although at first it may appear of little importance, yet by adducing one more to the already numerous examples will tend to generalise the law that the ova of all Zoophites enjoy spontaneous motion'. Darwin was already demonstrating two characteristic aspects of his research style: his acute observational skill and his mindfulness of the significance of single observations for theoretical generalisations.

Taxonomy did not interest him for its own sake. By 1844, Darwin had produced only one small addition to taxonomic literature, based on specimens collected during the *Beagle* voyage: he described several new species of terrestrial *Planaria* that he had discovered mostly in Chile and Brazil. In the introduction, Darwin focused on the differences between these land-living flatworms and their better-known marine counterparts, and he also noted that many of their adaptations to life on land were analogous to those of terrestrial gastropods. He concluded that the 'existence of

terrestrial Planariæ is analogous to that of terrestrial leeches in the forests of southern Chile and Ceylon'. Although Darwin had not mentioned transmutation, the subtext of a transformist view is apparent. The diagnostic features are not mere structural descriptions, rather they relate to the adaptation of each species to a particular way of life. If Darwin was going to embark on a larger taxonomic work, it was evident that it would be a taxonomy underpinned by the idea that the relationships among taxa were, in fact, evidence of true genealogical relatedness.

In his monograph, Darwin located the Cirripedia within the larger class of Crustacea and he located *Cryptophialus minutus* (the erstwhile 'Mr Arthrobalanus') within the Cirripedia. He demonstrated that a taxonomy that relied less on ideas about deviation from an ideal 'type' and more on the notion that structural changes were a response to changing ways of life could provide a system of classification that reflected material reality.

After the survey itself had been made, a 'rough' would have been drawn up, perhaps by the Assistant Surveyor, John Lort Stokes, working at the chart table in the poop cabin shared with Darwin. This would have undergone further improvement, and eventually a 'fair copy' been produced as the basis of the final engraved chart. As part of this process, tracings might be made of the draft charts, such as this one of the island of Chiloé now in the Cambridge University Library Darwin Archive, bearing an annotation in FitzRoy's hand: 'Excellent spot for a dock, RF'.

Surveying the Island of Chiloé

SIMON KEYNES

'Much interesting information has been acquired by my messmate Charles Darwin, in his wanderings ashore. He is a good pedestrian, as well as a good horseman; he is a sensible, shrewd, and sterling good fellow. While I am pottering about in the water, measuring depths and fixing positions, he wanders over the land, and frequently makes long excursions where I cannot go, because my duty is Hydro-not Geo-graphy.' (Robert FitzRoy to his sister Fanny, April 1834. See p. 23)

In early June 1834, Fitzroy took the *Beagle*, and her tender, the *Adventure*, from the Atlantic into the Strait of Magellan, along the Magdalen and Cockburn Channels, and out into the Pacific. The *Beagle*'s progress up the west coast was impeded by northerly gales, and FitzRoy decided to rest for several days (28 June–13 July) at San Carlos, in Chiloé, before proceeding onwards to Valparaiso.

Hydrography, which in this context meant the detailed examination of coastal waters, was indeed FitzRoy's duty. He was operating under instructions from the Admiralty 'to perform the operations and execute the surveys' as set out in a detailed memorandum drawn up by Francis Beaufort, who presided over the navy's Hydrographic Office. So, on reaching Valparaiso in late July 1834, Captain FitzRoy and his officers completed their work on the surveys of Patagonia, Tierra del Fuego, and the Falklands, and after several weeks were able to dispatch the finished charts back to England. It was also necessary for the ship's company to make ready the *Beagle*, and her boats, for the next stage in the surveying work, which would take them back to the south. Meanwhile, Darwin set off on his rambles.

In November 1834 the *Beagle* left Valparaiso (now without the *Adventure*, and also without Conrad Martens), in order to resume her work along the south-western coast. They were soon back in Chiloé, at a better season of the year; and while the *Beagle* herself surveyed the more exposed coasts, her boats worked in shallower waters and more confined spaces. FitzRoy gave his sister an account of what nearly became an international incident: it had emerged from the *Beagle's* survey that in the earlier, Spanish-made charts, the island of Chiloé appeared rather longer than it should. One of the *Beagle* crew remarked to a local inhabitant that, in their new survey, they had 'cut off twenty-five miles' of the island, but this was understood to mean that the English had taken possession of a large area, whereupon the islanders rose up in arms to support the English against the Spanish in what they took to be an attack on the Chilean mainland.

66 I continue to suffer so much from sea-sickness, that nothing, not even geology itself can make up for the misery & vexation of spirit. 99
Letter to Caroline Darwin, 10–13 March 1835

FitzRoy to his sister, Fanny: 'During the progress of our Survey we found that the Spaniards had (by some oversight) made the Island of Chiloé appear twenty five miles longer than the truth ...'

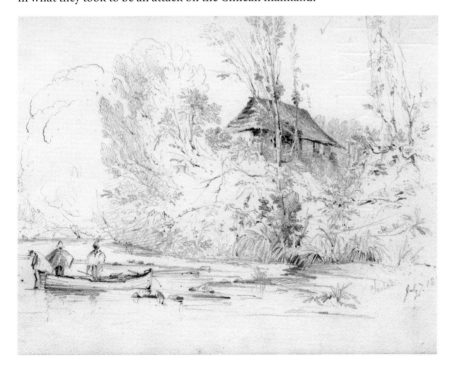

Surveying Chiloé. Conrad Martens, 7 July 1834

Curious formed valleys, petrified shells, volcanoes and strange scenery

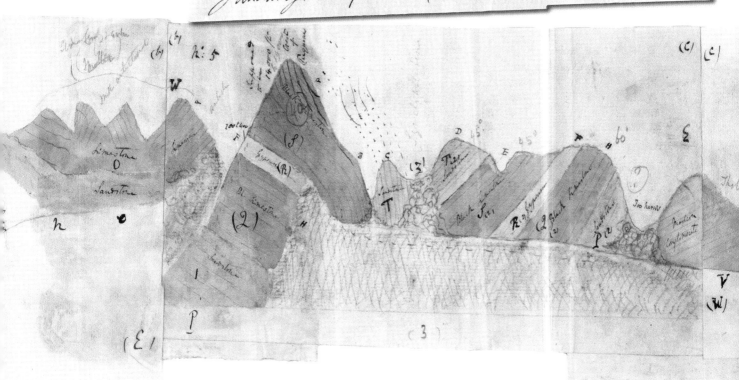

West coast inland expeditions to Andes; Peru. January – September 1835

Part of one of Darwin's composite geological cross-sections running west to east through the Portillo range of the Andes, Chile

The tedium was broken on 19 January 1835 when the volcano of Osorno erupted, and then just a month later a large section of the west coast was shaken by an earthquake. Darwin was in Valdivia where damage was relatively slight; further north in Concepción, which the *Beagle* reached on 4 March, they found much greater devastation – a tidal wave had engulfed the town and demolished almost every building.

As they moved north, Darwin did as he had done on the east coast, and made long inland expeditions. These were major undertakings. At twenty-five, often travelling without maps, and speaking little of the local language, he had learned to hire guides and horses, to arrange lodgings, get supplies, hunt for food, and cook his own meals. He set out from Santiago on horseback, to cross the Cordillera that he had explored from the east the year before, getting advice on the route from a settler,

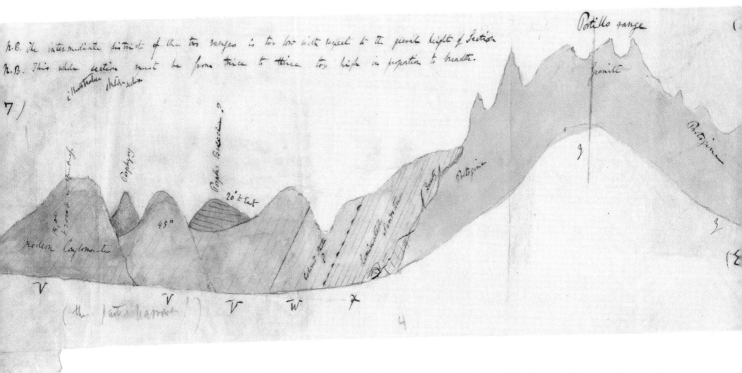

Alexander Caldcleugh, whose copper mines he visited. Going through the Uspallata pass, he encountered fossil trees, and was struck by the different plant and animal populations on either side of the mountains, despite the similarity of the conditions. He touched base briefly with the *Beagle* at Valparaiso before setting out again on a 220 mile ride through the Andes to Coquimbo and on to Copiapo. He joined the ship again to sail for Iquique in Peru, a short journey from Lima, which he reached at the end of July 1835.

ALISON M. PEARN

Thinking big: Darwin's geological cross-sections

Perhaps the most visually striking objects amongst Darwin's surviving papers from the *Beagle* voyage are a series of ten hand-coloured geological cross-sections. They range in size from fifteen centimetres to nearly two metres in width, and were pieced together from individual strips of paper. Darwin constructed them during the voyage based on the surface observations he made, and the mineral samples he collected in his inland expeditions: he was attempting to visualise the geological history of the entire sub-continent of South America, testing his field observations against the competing geological theories of the time and, increasingly, constructing his own grand concepts.

During his time in Cambridge, John Henslow and Adam Sedgwick had provided Darwin with the rudiments of rock and mineral identification. But he had also learned to see rocks at the small scale as representing geological features at the large scale, and in particular to interpret landscape by looking first at its subsurface structure.

In *Principles of Geology*, Charles Lyell argued against the 'catastrophist' interpretation of geology. Instead, he advocated that all features of the present day landscape could be explained as the result of the gradual operation over sufficient time of familiar geological processes, such as volcanism, sedimentation, erosion, subsidence and uplift.

Darwin, reading the *Principles* in instalments as the voyage progressed and newly published volumes reached him, was perfectly placed to test Lyell's assertions with firsthand observations made on a far larger scale than Lyell could at the time do himself.

Travelling north along the coast of Chile in the Spring of 1835, Darwin and FitzRoy were confronted with a series of violent natural events which they were perfectly placed to study. They witnessed the eruption of Mount Osorno, followed by an earthquake and tidal waves, the subsequent effects of which they witnessed at a

" I am glad to hear you have some thoughts of beginning geology. – I hope you will, there is so much larger a field for though, than in the other branches of Nat: history. – I am become a zealous disciple of Mr. Lyells views, as known in his admirable book. – Geologizing in S. America, I am tempted to carry parts to a greater extent, even than he does. "
Letter to W. D. Fox [9 – 12 August] 1835

One of Darwin's composite geological cross-sections of South America, from the west coast of Chile to the ridge of the Andes

The volcano of Osorno seen from Chiloé; Conrad Martens, July 1834

" I cannot tell you how I enjoyed some of these views. — it is worth coming from England once to feel such intense delight. At an elevation from 10 – 12000 feet. there is a transparency in the air & a confusion of distances & a sort of stillness which gives the sensation of being in another world, & when to this is joined, the picture so plainly drawn of the great epochs of violence, it causes in the mind a most strange assemblage of ideas. "

Letter to J. S. Henslow 18 April 1835

❝ *I have had ill luck however in only one little earthquake having happened. – I was lying in bed, when there was a party at dinner, in the house; on a sudden I heard such a hubbub in the dining room; without a word being spoken, it was devil take the hind most who should get out first: at the same moment I felt my bed slightly vibrate in a lateral direction. The party were old stagers & heard, the noise, which always precedes a shock; & no old Stager looks at an earthquake with philosophical eyes. ❞*
Letter to Catherine Darwin, 8 November 1834

number of points along their route. It was not just the large-scale devastation wreaked in the towns and villages that made an impression on them; they also noticed the small but measurable, and apparently permanent, effects on the land surface itself. FitzRoy was able to demonstrate by repeating his previous survey of 1834, that the surface of the land at Concepción had risen in altitude. He subsequently communicated these results to the Geological Society of London, much to Lyell's intense delight and vindication. Darwin, travelling inland, concluded that all these separate surface events could be explained by postulating shock waves from a single subterranean event. The more he examined the surface geology of the Andes in close detail, the more convinced he became that, vast though the mountain ranges were, they could be explained as the result of the repeated action of the same forces that he and FitzRoy had just witnessed. What struck him as he pored over his assembled cross-sections, was the uniformity of the geology of South America – the rocks that comprised the western slopes of the Andes followed the same order of stratification as those on the east, albeit fractured and distorted.

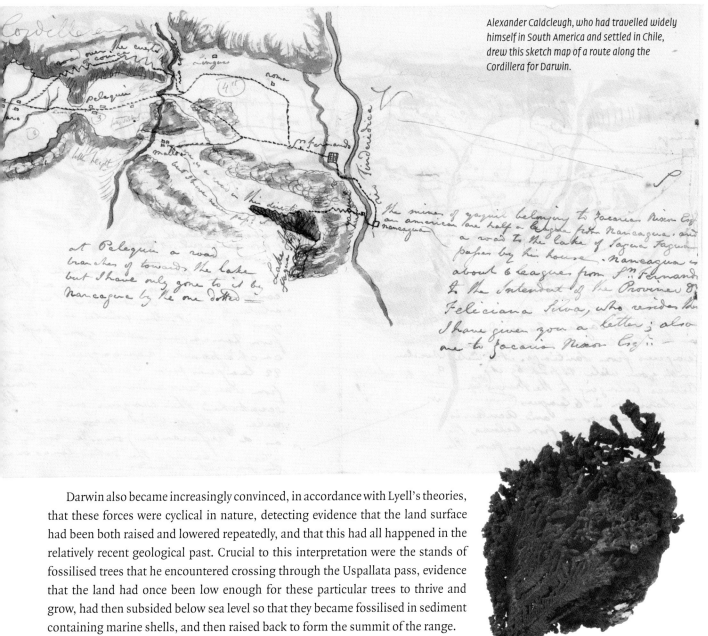

Alexander Caldcleugh, who had travelled widely himself in South America and settled in Chile, drew this sketch map of a route along the Cordillera for Darwin.

Native copper collected near Guasco, Chile, possibly from a mine belonging to Alexander Caldcleugh

Darwin also became increasingly convinced, in accordance with Lyell's theories, that these forces were cyclical in nature, detecting evidence that the land surface had been both raised and lowered repeatedly, and that this had all happened in the relatively recent geological past. Crucial to this interpretation were the stands of fossilised trees that he encountered crossing through the Uspallata pass, evidence that the land had once been low enough for these particular trees to thrive and grow, had then subsided below sea level so that they became fossilised in sediment containing marine shells, and then raised back to form the summit of the range.

Thinking on such a large scale, Darwin developed his own interpretation of the Earth's crust as huge sheets of rock – a similar concept to modern tectonic plates – that rose and fell as the molten material beneath heated and cooled, expanded and collapsed. Travelling on from South America and crossing back half way round the world, he began to apply this theory on a global scale. In his Red Notebook begun at sea in 1836, he jotted notes for himself for future publications, concluding that the 'Geology of whole world will turn out simple'.

LYALL I. ANDERSON

Fossil trees: Darwin's observations on geographical distribution on either side of the Cordillera

The fossilised remains of trees and wood have always been a great source of fascination. They provide a tangible link to the past through the shape and structure of an object with which we are all relatively familiar. We know what wood feels like and smells like, and how it can be fashioned and worked. To be faced with something that looks like wood, yet to find it converted into heavy, cold stone, invokes surprise and wonder, the more so when whole trees are found standing fossilised as if still growing.

Darwin collected a fair quantity of fossilised wood on his travels through South America, particularly in Argentina and Chile, and some of his specimens remain in the Beagle Collection at the Sedgwick Museum. He routinely referred to it as 'silicified wood', and in that description provided us with a vital clue as to the manner in which he believed the trees became fossilised.

Fossils represent dead plants and animals that fell to the ground or sea floor, were buried by successive waves of sediment and are now entombed in solid rock. The weight of overlying rock often squashes the remains flat, but wood converted to stone through a process known as 'permineralisation' retains its three-dimensionality. Permineralisation involves the gradual replacement of the fleeting, ephemeral organic tissue of the plant by hard durable minerals. The trunks of living trees are by their very nature superbly adapted conducting vessels, routinely transporting water from the roots to the leaves. Where tree trunks take up waters rich in minerals, or have groundwater pass through them after they are buried below the surface, minerals can be deposited and the wood turned to stone.

In silicified wood, the tissues and cell spaces are filled by the mineral silica, recognisable to us as the main constituent of sand. Silica is not normally soluble in water, at least not at ambient temperatures on the Earth's surface. It is only when water is heated to high temperature, as for example deep below the Earth's surface, and confined through the pressure of overlying rock, that silica enters into solution. It only crystallizes out when the water cools or the confining pressure is lowered, for example near or at the ground surface.

One of Darwin's earliest encounters with fossilised wood took place in South America on the Island of Chiloé, Chile, in December 1834. Here Darwin found some broken pieces which provided him with a section of a trunk 'in the direction of the medullary rays'. Whilst tree rings are concentric, medullary rays are the 'wheel spoke'-like structures radiating from the centre of a woody trunk to the outer edge. Often broken or incomplete fossil material provides more information than pristine whole objects,

Three specimens of fossilised wood collected by Darwin in Chile, one near Concepción (top), one when crossing the Andes (bottom left), and the other on the island of Chiloé (bottom right)

so it is reassuring to see that Darwin was methodically collecting representative samples and not just aesthetically pleasing trophies!

Why was Darwin interested in fossil wood? It was evidence of the past history of the region. In his notes, Darwin refers to dicotyledonous ('petrified Dycot wood') as well as to coniferous wood, showing that he was aware of the relatively recent age of the fossil vegetation. Flowering plants, of which dicotyledonous trees are a sub-set, first appeared during Cretaceous times, and their fossils therefore provide evidence for the maximum age of the enclosing rocks. Where he found the fossilised wood in association with other fossils such as marine shells, Darwin was able to divine something of the past juxtaposition of land and sea. Upright stumps of trees in sandy sediments of volcanic origin indicated the speed of burial of these remains, and the constituent minerals suggested possible fossilisation processes.

Darwin's notes on fossil wood from Chiloé

On 30 March 1835, Darwin marvelled at 'a petrified forest, fifty fossilized trunks in a sandstone escarpment' near the summit of the Uspallata Range. Here he compared the snow-white petrified trees to 'Lot's Wife' from the Biblical account, but importantly noted that 'close to the trees is a broad metallic dyke' or as we now understand it, a metal ore vein. A gold mine had been opened nearby to exploit this vein. His notebooks and a letter to John Henslow suggest that Darwin viewed the economic mineral geology and the close proximity of the fossil trees as no mere coincidence. The same mineral-rich fluids may have been responsible for the formation of both phenomena. Recent research now dates these coniferous trees as being of Triassic age, significantly older than the Tertiary age Darwin originally suggested. A few days later, on 5 April 1835, Darwin encountered a massive fossilised tree lying horizontal amidst sedimentary conglomerate rock. This sufficiently stirred his imagination to make him visualize a former world:

A drawer of thin sections taken from Beagle specimens over the years at the Sedgwick Museum of Earth Sciences, Cambridge. As well as sections of fossil wood, these include sections from the St Paul's Rocks specimens

> 'I can show that this grand chain consisted of Volcanic Islands, covered with luxurious forests; some of the trees, one of 15 ft in circumference, I have seen silicified & imbedded in marine strata.'

A later derivative of the Beagle Collection consists of prepared microscope slides made from the rocks. Within this collection are two slides of fossil wood, BC 1573 from Santa Fe, Bajada, Argentina, and BC 2703 collected from the Santiago–Mendoza traverse. Microscope examination of BC 2703 reveals the permineralizing mineral in this fossil as calcite (calcium carbonate) rather than silica as Darwin had described.

Overall, the fossil trees provided Darwin with further evidence of the veracity of Charles Lyell's thoughts on the continuation of geological processes up until the present time. That a modern species of tree could be fossilised in the same manner as species long extinct revealed the uniformity of earth processes.

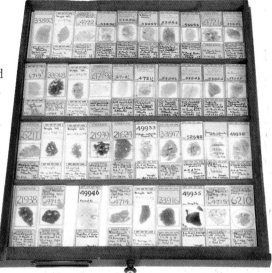

University Museum of Zoology Cambridge: The Darwin collections

ADRIAN FRIDAY

ARGUS PHEASANT
Argusianus argus

Wing feathers, showing the differentiation of ocelli.
These are the specimens described by Darwin.
See *The Descent of Man*, 2nd ed pp. 434 et seq.
PRESENTED BY PROFESSOR G H DARWIN, 1904

On his return from the *Beagle* voyage, Darwin spent several months in a house at 22 Fitzwilliam Street, Cambridge, dividing his zoological specimens into lots to be sent to appropriate taxonomic specialists all over the country. Then, as now, some of the specialists who received specimens were more efficient in completing their descriptions, and more careful with the material, than others.

Today, in addition to the collection in the University Museum of Zoology in Cambridge, there are notable holdings of *Beagle* specimens in The Natural History Museum, London, the Oxford University Museum of Natural History, and the Rijksmuseum, Leiden.

The zoological material collected by Charles Darwin housed in the University Museum of Zoology Cambridge, falls into three groups: insects collected while Darwin was an undergraduate at Christ's College; material from the voyage of HMS *Beagle*; and the barnacle specimens on microscope slides prepared by Darwin when he was producing his monograph on barnacles. The barnacle material dates from Darwin's studies between 1846 and 1854.

The *Beagle* material was not acquired as a single collection, but arrived over an extended period. During the voyage Darwin sent back some specimens to England, notably to John Stevens Henslow. Some of the material that Henslow received came to the University Museum of Zoology by way of the Cambridge Philosophical Society; other components of the present holdings were acquired later. The Museum's share of the famous finches from the Galápagos Islands, for example, comprise seven specimens that had passed through the hands of the ornithologist John Gould (1804–1881), together with one additional specimen that was acquired separately. A quantity of taxonomically very diverse invertebrate specimens came to the Museum in 1870, by the agency of Darwin's son, Francis, then an undergraduate at Trinity College, and later instrumental in the transfer of the barnacle material.

Early beetle collection and Beagle aquatic insects

The University Museum of Zoology's Register for April 1913 records the following acquisition:

> 'Small collection of British beetles, made by Charles Darwin. The beetles were originally in a cabinet, until in the early '70s G.R. Crotch removed some or all of them into boxes, with the intention of arranging and renaming them. Only one box has been found, which was given to the Museum as Crotch left it, some of the beetles being named in Crotch's handwriting, others with printed labels. Whether the latter were Darwin's or Crotch's naming is not known. Donated by Sir Francis Darwin, F.R.S.'

The box of beetles is currently exhibited in the University Museum of Zoology's own display of Darwin's specimens, and is a very concrete link with Darwin's fanatical insect collecting in the period shortly before he became a recruit for naturalist on the *Beagle*.

'More like a work of art than of nature' (Darwin, Descent of Man 1871)
Darwin concluded that the beautiful markings on the wing feathers of male Argus pheasants had been developed through sexual selection. Darwin's collection of feathers was given to the University Museum of Zoology Cambridge by his son George.

Preservation – then and now

Darwin used a variety of techniques for preservation of his material. The beetles collected by the undergraduate Darwin, were pinned, with labels, in the conventional manner still much used today.

The *Beagle* specimens, both invertebrate and vertebrate, were generally preserved in alcohol, and some were later dried.

The barnacle specimens, from the period closer to the publication of *Origin*, consist chiefly of parts of the barnacles mounted on microscope slides.

Each of these different forms of preservation brings its own problems for previous and current generations of curators.

Most of the material has survived very well, but some of the *Beagle* invertebrates received after Darwin's death were found to have deteriorated and, sadly, were destroyed very early in the 20th century. Also, the barnacle specimens have in many cases suffered the fate of most early preparations for microscopic examination, with the 'creeping', over the years, of the semi-viscous varnishes (gold size or asphalt) used to seal the mounts.

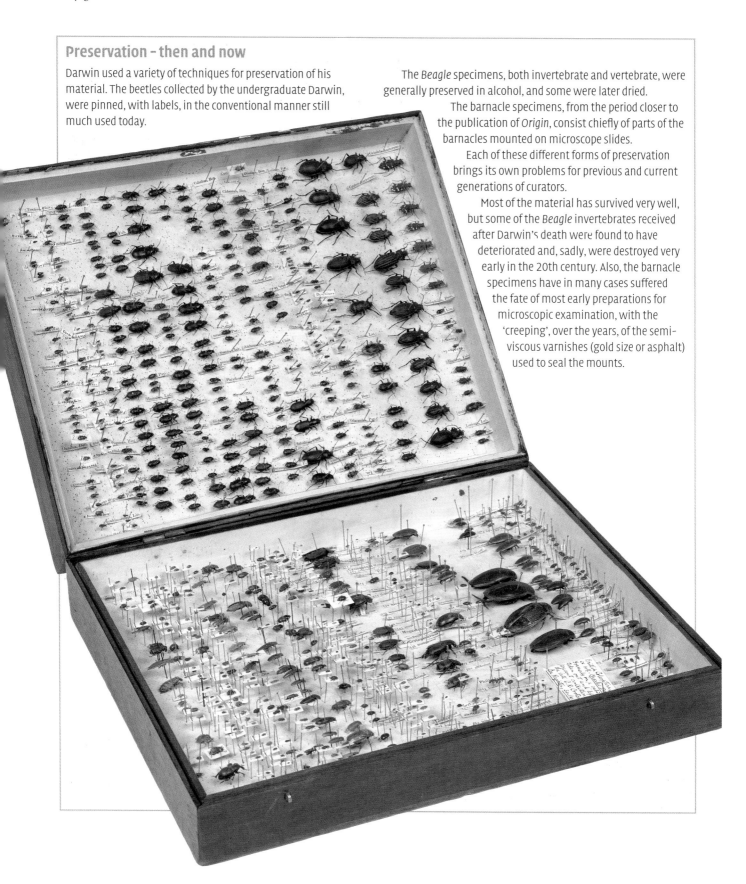

The Museum also has a small number of water beetles and bugs from the *Beagle* voyage. These came to the collections by way of Professor Charles Babington (1808–95) who had received them from Darwin after the voyage. Babington's description of the material was published in 1842.

Beagle finches (see pp. 94–95)

The finches from the Galápagos Islands have become iconic specimens. Their history, however, has been convoluted. Meticulous work by Frank Sulloway cleared away much of the overheated mythology surrounding the inspiration Darwin supposedly drew from his knowledge of the finches. Even the colloquial names for the birds, either 'Galápagos finches' or 'Darwin's finches', are unfortunate: the former because the subfamily Geospizinae has members that occur outside the Galápagos Islands, and the latter because it suggests that the finches were pivotal to the development of Darwin's evolutionary thought. Sulloway demonstrated that the Darwin of the *Beagle* years was not an especially erudite ornithologist; he was a less than meticulous recorder of localities for the birds, having to reconstruct these well after collection when he was back in England, and his use of the finches in his later thought and writing was very limited (partly because he seemed always to have doubts about the accuracy of the attributions). Perhaps the most telling truth is that the finches were not mentioned in *Origin of Species*. The finches are indeed important as an example of an adaptive radiation (of some complexity) and of evolutionary processes, but that importance has been acquired as a result of much distinguished work after Darwin's own time. So pervasive is the 'well known' importance of the finches to Darwin that he is often credited with observations and discoveries made well after his death. It is probably reasonable to suggest, as Sulloway does, that Darwin was able to interpret the finches in the light of his evolutionary ideas, rather than the other way round.

The *Beagle* finch specimens in the University Museum of Zoology were not in fact collected by Darwin himself, but by Harry Fuller, who was personal steward to Captain FitzRoy. During the voyage Darwin certainly did collect some finch specimens, but so also did his own assistant, Syms Covington – and Fitzroy, and Fuller. Indeed, it was the recording of localities of collection by these others that made it possible for Darwin to reconstruct missing locality data for the finches after the voyage. Fuller's collection appears to have included eight of the finches; and they retain labels that locate them in FitzRoy's catalogue of specimens. Additional labels have enabled the establishment of the history of the specimens after the voyage. Fuller's specimens were either given or sold to Dr Armstrong of the Haslar Museum, part of the Royal Naval Hospital in Plymouth. When this Museum closed in 1856, the Admiralty presented most of the material to the British Museum, but seven of Fuller's finches came into the hands of the naturalist Sir William Jardine (1800–74), who added his own labels. After Jardine's death his collection was sold by auction in 1886 and the Cambridge ornithologist, Alfred Newton, bought the seven finches for the University Museum of Zoology.

But Fuller had collected eight finches. The eighth came to Cambridge as part of the H.E. Strickland bequest. Hugh Edwin Strickland (1811–53) was a highly regarded gentleman biologist who met an untimely death as a result of being hit by a train while geologizing in a railway cutting – for a naturalist perhaps simultaneously tragic and fitting. Among that collection was Fuller's eighth finch. Strickland's label indicates that his possession of the specimen was expedited by Darwin, who must have got the bird from Fuller (perhaps via FitzRoy).

Frank Sulloway was able to collate all available information for the eight Cambridge specimens collected by Fuller. All of these birds were described by the ornithologist John Gould (of the Zoological Society of London) and are therefore of substantial taxonomic importance. They fall into five species as described by Gould. Particularly notable is one male specimen of the species *Geospiza magnirostris*, the large-billed form. This specimen has the largest bill of all similar specimens collected on the *Beagle* voyage. Fuller, the original collector, and Jardine, the subsequent owner of seven of the birds, had their own difficulties with both sexing and naming the specimens: it was not until well into the second half of the 20th century that localities, sexes, identification and nomenclature came together for the finch specimens in Cambridge.

The University Museum of Zoology, Cambridge, has several other birds from the *Beagle* voyage, including a steamer duck, *Tachyeres patachonicus* (*Tachyeres brachypterus*; see p.54). This was one of the specimens that Darwin himself brought back to England on the *Beagle* (most of his own other bird specimens were sent back during the voyage to Henslow for storage). The duck was one of a number of birds then sent to Darwin's friend Thomas Eyton in Shropshire. Eyton wrote an anatomical appendix to the 1841 account of the *Beagle* birds, by Gould and others.

Some of Darwin's Beagle fish specimens still preserved in the University Museum of Zoology Cambridge

Francis Darwin (1848–1925)

Known to his family as 'Frank', Charles Darwin's seventh child, who was so important in expediting the Cambridge acquisition of important material left after his father's death, himself became a distinguished scientist. He was an undergraduate at Trinity College, Cambridge, initially studying mathematics, but then transferring to natural sciences. Subsequently he studied medicine in London, but never practised. He was elected to the Royal Society in 1882, the year of his father's death. From 1884 until his resignation in 1904, he taught botany in Cambridge. He was knighted in 1913, the year of his third marriage (his first two wives having died, and his third wife predeceased him). It is noteworthy, of course, that his father had not been knighted, although in 1877 Charles Darwin was awarded an honorary degree from the University of Cambridge. Francis had worked with his father, notably on movement in plants, and they had written a book on this topic together (the 1880 *The Power of Movement in Plants*). Perhaps Francis Darwin, whom the family regarded as a talented writer, is mostly remembered today for his attention to his father's reputation: in 1887 he had published an edited version of his father's autobiography, and in the same year, and again in 1905, he published volumes of Charles's selected letters. His Royal Society obituary notice suggests a gifted, straightforward and deeply kind man.

A F

As late as several years ago, a further *Beagle* bird specimen (a giant petrel, *Macronectes gigantea*, known to Darwin as *Procellaria gigantea*) was identified as such in the University Museum of Zoology (by Clem Fisher of World Museum Liverpool). As Frank Steinheimer has observed, almost half the number of bird specimens collected by Darwin on the voyage cannot now be accounted for (despite the fact that *Beagle* birds are known from eight different institutions). Perhaps there are still discoveries to be made.

Beagle fish

The fish specimens from the *Beagle* voyage were sent for description to Leonard Jenyns, an old friend of Darwin's who was vicar of Swaffham Bulbeck, near Cambridge. Jenyns did a magnificent job with the material, and after his death the fish, mostly preserved in alcohol, but a few dried, came to the University Museum of Zoology along with many of Jenyns's scientific papers, including his manuscript *Notes on the Fishes collected by Chas Darwin in the Voyage of HMS Beagle*. More than 60 specimens of *Beagle* fish remain in the Museum, despite the transfer of a substantial number to The Natural History Museum, London, in 1917. (See pp.110–12)

Beagle invertebrates

A diverse collection of *Beagle* invertebrate specimens in alcohol, given to the Museum by Darwin and delivered in 1870 by the undergraduate Francis Darwin, was definitively curated in 1901 with the benefit of Darwin's original manuscript catalogue, lent by Francis Darwin. A number of specimens had deteriorated in preservation and were destroyed, but most were conserved and dispersed, according to group, in the general collections. There were sponges, sea anemones and corals, nematode worms, an arrow worm, leech, and polychaete worms, sipunculan worms, molluscs, bryozoans, brittle stars and sea cucumbers, and sea squirts.

The University Museum of Zoology's Annual Report for 1901 gives details of the curation, noting that 'In one or two cases these specimens are important in consequence of being referred to (without determination) in the pages of the *Beagle* 'Journal'. I am informed by a chemical friend that the metal labels are made of tin. It is worthy of notice that their distinctiveness has in no way been impaired by an immersion of seventy years in weak spirit.'

The University Museum of Zoology has a substantial holding of bryozoan specimens collected by Darwin on the *Beagle* voyage, including those important in the development of Darwin's ideas about the evolution of bryozoan morphology.

Plate I (Balanus tintinnabulum) from Charles Darwin, A mongraph on the subclass Cirripedia: Balanidae *(1854)*

BALANUS TINTINNABULUM.

George Sowerby

Barnacles

Darwin worked on barnacles (*Cirripedia*) between 1846 and 1854. Eight years may sound like a long time, but Darwin had to solicit specimens from all over the world to add to those he had collected himself – some from the *Beagle* voyage – and to carry out some very demanding micro-dissection. There is still controversy over what motivated Darwin: was the multi-volume monograph on the Cirripedia to prove his taxonomic credentials? Did Darwin feel the need to look at one group (any group, perhaps) in great detail to test some of his ideas? Or was he deliberately passing the time, albeit fruitfully, in order to delay the publication of his work on natural selection? Each of these theories has its supporters and opponents. Perhaps he was simply fascinated by barnacles.

The University Museum of Zoology has most of the slides prepared by Darwin during this work, together with his hand-written list of the material, where he details 285 items. The Darwin scholar (and co-founding editor of the Darwin Correspondence Project), the late Sydney Smith, had established that the paper of Darwin's list closely resembles the paper used for his 'Big book' *Natural Selection*, the never completed full version of *Origin*, begun in 1856: there is no reason to suppose that the list of slides was not made at the time of their preparation. The slides appear to have been, characteristically, a means to an end. They are not elegantly prepared; but, even now, they do give the impression of work in progress.

For such facts would undermine the stability of species

Finches (Geospizinae) collected in the Galápagos during the Beagle voyage (see pp. 97–8). These are all 'type specimens', that is, they are the individual birds from which the description of each species was originally established.

The Galápagos Islands,
September 1835 - October 1835

After a few weeks re-stocking with supplies near Lima, the *Beagle* struck west to explore the Pacific islands, and on 15 September 1835, they dropped anchor off the Galápagos Islands.

DAVID KOHN

Silent species: South American Beagle collections and the origins of Darwin's species theory

By the end of the *Beagle* voyage, Darwin's natural history collections had provided him with the first evidence for the 'species theory' that would define his life's work. But instances of Darwin writing in a theoretical mode about species during the voyage are sparse. This has contributed to the false impression that Darwin 'merely' amassed specimens in South America, later sifted for new species by experts in England. But if we catch the rhythm of his thinking about species during the continental years of relative silence, then the first emergence of Darwin's theory near the end of the voyage is more intelligible.

Species concept

The very clear species concept embodied in John Stevens Henslow's herbarium collection was communicated to Darwin at Cambridge. That creationist concept recognized the 'reality' and 'stability', but also the variability, of immutable species. Henslow determined the limits of a species by comparing geographic variants laid side by side. The implicit question is always: 'are these species or are they varieties?' We find Darwin asking this question in March 1833 while collecting gastropods on East Falkland Island: 'two specimens of same genus: but I think different species. Are these Species or Varieties?' Two specimens of the birds he called *Certhia* provoked the same question in Maldonado, May–June 1833, as did Chilean land slugs collected in 1834.

Darwin encountered the same concept of limited variation from type when the second volume of Charles Lyell's *Principles of Geology* reached Monte Video in November 1832. Just a month before, Darwin collected a hefty, bony-cased mammalian fossil (*Glyptodon*) at Bahia Blanca, which he intuitively related to the armadillos now living there 'in very great numbers'. Later, Darwin was to transform the relation between living and extinct animals in the same location into a relationship, as Lyell put it, between 'the birth and death of species'. During the voyage, this line of thought culminated in February 1835 in Chile, where Darwin wrote tantalizingly: 'The following analogy I am aware is a false one; but when I consider the enormous extension of life of an *individual* plant, seen in the grafting of an Apple tree, & that all these thousand trees are subject to the duration of life which one bud contained. I cannot see such difficulty in believing a similar duration might be propagated by true generation'. These passages point almost verbatim to explicitly evolutionary passages in Darwin's Red Notebook, written in London in 1837. While these powerfully cognate passages – both referring to the extinction of the same animal (the Port St Julian 'mastodon', later identified by Richard Owen as an extinct guanaco, *Macrauchenia*) do not mean that Darwin was already an evolutionist in Chile, they do lead to a dramatic conclusion that Darwin scholars have long urged: Darwin of the *Beagle*, through his intense reading of Lyell, was overtly struggling with transformism for six months before he even stepped onto the Galápagos.

Darwin's Rhea (Rhea pennata)

Representative species

With respect to geographic distribution, Lyell both reinforced and extended what Henslow had taught Darwin. Whereas Henslow discussed Alexander von Humboldt's botanical regions 'enclosing particular species ... so encompassed by physical obstructions, that the great majority of species found within their limits are not to be met with elsewhere', Lyell based his biogeography on the idea of representative species promoted by Georges-Louis Leclerc, the Comte de Buffon. 'In Peru and Chili ... crowds of lama, guanaco, and alpaca ... represent the genus camel of the ancient continent ...' 'Related' but different representatives are found in different regions of the world.

For both Henslow and Lyell, biogeographic ideas supported immutable species. Distribution took place by 'gradual dispersion from one definite spot on the earth's surface', their unique centre of creation. Later in his halcyon London days Darwin, already a transformist, ratcheted the frame of reference down from Buffon's large regional, intercontinental comparisons to a much more localised focus on the succession of closely related representative species that replace each other in adjoining territories on a continent.

But Darwin did not make this characteristically 'Darwinian' move while on the *Beagle*. If we look closely at the silent record of Darwin's collection, we do not find the idea of a replacement series or of representative species. Instead, when it comes to those birds of particular interest, the mocking birds, we find quite the opposite! In retrospect, we can see that the material was there. Darwin later, following Alcide d'Orbigny, recognised several species of the mocking thrush genus in his South American collections. But during the *voyage* Darwin lumped mocking birds into a catchall group he calls *Lanius*, a genus in the shrike family: 'This bird has a wide geographical range, being found wherever the country is open & tolerably dry. On the east coast I met with it everywhere from Lat: 31°. to 50° in Southern Patagonia; On the West coast it is likewise abundant from Lima (12°) to Concepción (37°)'. We can see how Darwin relies on Buffonian representation, for his '*Lanius*', which doesn't exist in South America, is a token 'representative' name. But he just didn't know ornithology deeply enough to identify, let alone detect multispecies distribution patterns in, these unfamiliar South American birds.

Peculiarity

From both Henslow and Lyell, Darwin had absorbed the concept of peculiarity or endemism. This is the idea that some species occur in only one place in the world. The most famous case is the two *Rheas*. At Rio Negro in August 1833, Darwin 'heard much concerning the 'Avestruz petises'' as the Gauchos termed them, and in December 1833 recorded reports of 'a second species of Rhea. – which is very rarely found N of the R. Negro. – ' Here are two close species with adjacent and perhaps even overlapping distributions; one is an endemic, confined to the southern slice of Patagonia. Darwin famously took this case up again in the Red Notebook in 1837. Not so the black Falkland rabbit, whose identity 'as a distinct species, the Lepus Magellanicus' he denied. At the same time, in March 1834, he accepted the Falkland fox as a distinct species from the continental form, the product as he put it, 'of what appears to me to be a centre of creation'. This is a palpable indication that he had not yet strayed from Henslow and Lyell. But he goes further with this species, adding a note to suggest that there are distinct East Island and West Island Falkland foxes. These would be endemic island varieties of an endemic species.

Galápagos ho!

We cannot know the state of Darwin's thinking when he landed in the Galápagos in September 1835. But we have seen that there were several traces in his South American notes of specific issues that would later feed directly into his first 1837 crafting of the species theory: the overlapping *Rhea* species of the Rio Negro, the mammals that may have gone extinct without a physical change in their environment, the very template used in pursuing the species theory – namely Darwin's organizing idea that the laws of ordinary reproduction might be applied to understand the 'birth' of species. All this may have meant nothing in particular to him until ... well, until 'later'. But two things we can know with some confidence to have been part of his mental mix in September 1835. First, he had thought intensely about Lyell's species ideas in February 1835. But Lyell's critique of Lamarckian transformist theory had not completely convinced him; since he could not have thought this through without also thinking about transmutation, that issue was 'there' too, even though its trace is largely silent. Second, he landed on Chatham Island having concluded that all the South American mocking birds were but one species.

So it is quite wonderful that in what seems to have been his first walkabout on Chatham, he should have encountered 'Thencas', that is, mocking birds (*Galápagos Notebook*). And he concluded that here too they were part of the same species. Ornithologically, Galápagos appeared to be part of the South American biogeographic region. At the same time he asked whether a botanist would recognize these islands as South American. The implied answer was no, the Galápagos is its own botanical region, where he could expect to find endemic

> In September we leave the coast of America: & my Father will believe, that I will not draw money in crossing the Pacific, because I can not. – I verily believe I could spend money in the very moon.
>
> Letter to Susan Darwin, 23 April 1835

plant species. Thereafter, he systematically collected all Galápagos plants he found in flower.

That expectation would have been founded on Henslow's lectures. But it would have been reinforced by the endemics he had already paid attention to in South America – the Avestruz Petisse and the Falkland fox. Therefore, it is exceedingly important that we not rip Darwin's next move out of the botanico–zoological context in which it arose. That next move was to go to Charles Island, where he of course continued to collect for botanical endemics and to keep an eye out for Thencas. According to Darwin's post-*Beagle* accounts, which sound convincingly like recollections of real events, he immediately found a distinctly different mocking bird. The most striking is in the *Zoology of the 'Beagle'*, 3: 63: 'I fortunately happened to observe, that the specimens which I collected in the two first islands we visited, differed from each other, and this made me pay particular attention to their collection.' So, it was on Charles that the mocking birds escaped the halo of South America and thus came into conformity with the endemic peculiarity of the plants.

Darwin apparently first wrote up his Galápagos ornithological observations shortly after leaving the archipelago:

> *This bird which is so closely allied to the Thenca of Chili (Callandra of B. Ayres) is singular from existing as varieties or distinct species in the different Isds. – I have four specimens from as many Isds. – These will be found to be 2 or 3 varieties. – Each variety is constant in its own Island. –*

Darwin is asking the same question as always. Are these birds varieties or species? And for the very first time on the voyage Darwin had observed up to three distinct varieties/species in a defined geographical relationship. This then is the first geographical series he witnessed: Chatham, Charles, James. He clearly realizes there is something 'singular' in this case, which he notes seems comparable to the eye-witness report that distinct Tortoises come from different islands. Especially since he continued to equate Thenca and Callandra across a whole continent, for him suddenly to find distinct varieties or species, each 'constant in its own Island' made the archipelago indeed 'singular'.

There is no evidence however that this singularity had yet caused Darwin to depart from Henslow's creationist species concept. That happened some eight months later when he was half a world away in the Atlantic. We do not know what species thoughts came to Darwin as the *Beagle* ploughed the Pacific, Indian, and Atlantic oceans. We do know that he made reading notes on examples of endemism in isolated floras. In about July 1836, Darwin and his servant copied out all his zoological and botanical notes by major taxonomic group. In his *Ornithological Notes* he copied and amplified his treatment of the Galápagos mocking birds. The facts, of course, hadn't changed, just what he made of them. One important difference is that to the Tortoise comparison he now added the Falkland fox: 'The only fact of a similar kind of which I am aware, is the constant asserted difference – between the wolf-like Fox of East & West Falkland Islds.' This is fascinating because the difference between the East Island and West Island foxes is at the level of variety. Then came the famous show stopper: 'If there is the slightest foundation for these remarks the zoology of Archipelagoes – will be well worth examining; for such facts would undermine the stability of Species.'

Darwin's ornithological notes from the Galápagos, including the words 'such facts would undermine the stability of Species'

This marks the point where Darwin broke with the creationist species concept that Henslow taught him, that Lyell injected into the transformist debate, and that had guided his scientific practice throughout South America. It didn't happen on the rugged Galápagos. Rather more plausibly, it happened just before Darwin took his place in English scientific society – with a nascent theory in his head, and a notebook in his hand.

Mus. Henslow.

SPECIMEN COLLECTED BY CHARLES DARWIN
ON THE VOYAGE OF THE 'BEAGLE'
DEC. 27. 1831 — OCT. 2. 1836

UNIVERSITY HERBARIUM
BOTANY SCHOOL, DOWNING ST.
CAMBRIDGE   ENGLAND

Cambridge University Herbarium

00353 (CGE)

HOLOTYPE

Sicyos villosa Hooker fil.

Trans. Linn. Soc. London 20: 223 (1847).

Sicyos villosa, Hook fil

Galapagos; S. Amer:
(Charles Island)
Sept 1835 C. Darwin.
in great beds injurious to vegetation

Sicyos villosa: from abundance to extinction

When Darwin landed on Charles Island (Isla Santa Maria) on 23 September 1835 he was struck by the sight of a scrambling vine apparently suffocating the rest of the flora. He remarks that it was 'in great beds injurious to vegetation'. This rampant plant was a member of the family Cucurbitaceae, the squashes and cucumbers. It had a rough, ridged stem and broad leaves, and clambered over other vegetation, attaching itself by numerous tendrils. This pernicious plant was subsequently described by Joseph Hooker as a new species of the widespread Pacific and Australian genus *Sicyos*, which he called *S. villosa*. The specific name refers to its coating of rough, shaggy hairs.

Remarkably, this species was never collected again, nor was it noted by later visitors to the island. It is extinct today, and we presume that it died out soon after Darwin's visit. It was perhaps particularly abundant and lush when Darwin saw it since he remarks that there had been 'an unusual quantity of rain at this time of year'. Its demise may have been due to the 'wild pigs and goats which abound' on the island, providing fresh meat for the penal colony and for passing ships.

The only record we have of this intriguing species is the single sheet in Henslow's herbarium. It is thus the type specimen of an extinct species.

JP

I hope my wanderings will not unfit me for a quiet life

Tahiti, Australia, New Zealand, Indian Ocean islands; round the Cape of Good Hope; Atlantic islands; back to Brazil; home, November 1835 – October 1836

On 20 October 1835, after a stay of five weeks, the *Beagle* left the Galápagos bound for Tahiti, where FitzRoy had official business with the queen, and on 23 November Darwin got his first chance to examine a coral reef. After a stay of only a week, they headed west again bound for New Zealand where they spent Christmas. The New Zealand stay was also short with little time for exploration, but Darwin was struck by the fact that there was only one indigenous mammal - a rat - and, piecing together his observations since first landfall in St Jago, was deeply pondering the origin of island populations. Arriving in Australia early in January 1836, Darwin and FitzRoy visited Conrad Martens who had set up in business in Sydney and both commissioned finished watercolours from him based on original sketches he had made while with the *Beagle*. Darwin bought two, and once again wrote guiltily to his father about the extra expense.

Papetoai, Tahiti. Conrad Martens

Papetoai
Jun 29

Homeward bound

Darwin, now twenty-six, had been away from home for four and a half years – already twice as long as originally planned. He was able to make further careful observations of coral reefs at Keeling Island in April, and was intrigued when they landed briefly at Cape Town to meet the explorer and zoologist Andrew Smith, and the famous astronomer John Herschel, who was there to observe Halley's comet. Both men corresponded with Darwin for the rest of their lives. There were more observations of island habitats at St Helena and Ascension Island, but his main occupation was long hours going over his notes and writing them up more fully. At last the *Beagle* seemed to be heading back to England, but there was one more detour in store. FitzRoy had detected some inconsistencies in the charts made on the very first leg of the journey off the coast of Brazil, and, to Darwin's disgust, decided to return to take the soundings again. Jaded and ready for home, Darwin found even the Cape Verde islands far less exciting on a second visit. Finally, on 2 October 1836, after a voyage of 4 years, 9 months, and 6 days, the *Beagle* sailed into Falmouth harbour.

Trunks and barrels full of specimens had preceded Darwin and were keeping a number of his scientific colleagues occupied. Excerpts from his letters published by Henslow had already established his reputation. Over the next ten years, his notes and diaries furnished him with the raw material for more than twenty articles, for his contributions to *The Zoology of the voyage of HMS Beagle*, which he edited, and for *Journal of Researches*, an entertaining account of the voyage which became one of the world's best-selling travel books. Notebooks begun in the months immediately after the voyage show Darwin already beginning to think along the lines that led ultimately to the ideas published in *On the Origin of Species*.

Crociodolite presented to Darwin in Cape Town, South Africa by Andrew Smith (top), and volcanic olivine basalt with mineral-filled cavities (amygdaloids), from Tahiti, November, 1835

Darwin and coral reefs   ALISTAIR SPONSEL

When the *Beagle* departed Britain, Captain FitzRoy carried a set of orders from the Admiralty that dictated exactly where and how his survey should be carried out. He was also instructed to make a more general investigation of a phenomenon that had been terrifying European navigators for more than a century, the treacherously low islands that we now call atolls. FitzRoy was told to exert 'every means ... that ingenuity can devise' to determine the origin of the 'circularly formed Coral Islands in the Pacific.' Recent voyagers had declared these ring-shaped reefs to be formed by shallow water animals that could only live within thirty feet of sea level, but somehow they grew up in parts of the ocean that were so deep as to be literally unfathomable with the lengths of rope usually carried by explorers. The solution to this apparent paradox, endorsed at the time by everyone from Charles Lyell to Francis Beaufort, was that these so-called 'lagoon islands' must be formed atop volcano craters lying at depths of less than thirty feet. Beaufort's instructions to FitzRoy called this a 'modern and very plausible theory.' Yet by the end of the voyage, Darwin had rejected it as 'a monstrous hypothesis' and developed a new theory that helped to make him a scientific celebrity.

Darwin's initial interest in reefs was fuelled by his study of living corals, which were classed among the plant-like animals then known as zoophytes. During the first three years of the *Beagle* voyage Darwin spent so much of his time studying the (non-reef forming) corals of South American waters that he came to view them as his zoological speciality. The notes of Darwin's coral dissections in the Cambridge archives affirm what he wrote, with ever-idiosyncratic spelling, to his sister

Catherine in July 1834: 'I have lately determined to work chiefly amongst the Zoophites or Coralls: it is an enormous branch of the organized world; very little known or arranged & abounding with most curious, yet simple, forms of structures.' He boasted that he had already uncovered major flaws in the coral classifications made by the century's greatest naturalists, Lamarck and Cuvier, but he could hardly wait to depart South America and examine the 'Corall reefs & various animals of the Pacific,' for he found that 'the very thoughts of the fine Coralls, the warm glowing weather, the blue sky of the Tropics is enough to make one wild with delight.'

It was in the tropical Pacific, at the island of Tahiti, that Darwin realised he could revise the common understanding of coral formations as well as the taxonomy of coral animals. As he confided to his diary, 'It is my opinion, that besides the avowed ignorance concerning the tiny architects of each individual species, little is yet known, in spite of the much which has been written, of the structure & origin of the Coral Islands & reefs.' The crucial moment occurred on 17 November 1835, when Darwin, after climbing to an elevation of three thousand feet, beheld the neighbouring island of Eimeo (now called Moorea). Eimeo jutted from the Pacific in a mass of 'lofty & broken peaks,' but it was encircled by a lagoon of calm water, and beyond that by a reef identical to that of an atoll, which appeared as a 'well defined line of brilliant white where the waves first encountered the wall of coral.' From this startling vantage point, Darwin wrote, 'I was forcibly struck with this opinion ... Remove the central group of mountains, & there remains a Lagoon Is[land].' He already had an idea of how the mountainous island might be removed from the picture, because he had decided earlier in the year that the floor of the Pacific must have subsided in order to compensate for the adjacent bulging of the earth that had raised the continent of South America. While the *Beagle* sailed on from Tahiti to New Zealand in December 1835, Darwin sat aboard and wrote out a twenty-page essay that disposed of the crater-rim hypothesis.

Darwin's 'Coral Islands' manuscript of late 1835 argued that atolls were remnants formed when high islands sank and coral reefs that had formed in the shallow waters along their shore grew upward so that their tops remained near sea level. As long as the subsidence proceeded slowly or infrequently so that the living

" is a most comfortable reflection to me, that a ship being made of wood & iron, cannot last for ever & therefore this voyage must have an end. "

J. S. Henslow, 24 July – 7 November 1834

corals never dropped below the depth where they could flourish, the reef would persist even while the central island receded. Eventually this process would create a vista like Eimeo, where a barrier reef of living coral stood away from shore at such a distance that its dead foundation, the former shore reef, must now lie well beneath the crucial thirty-foot depth limit. If the subsidence continued for so long that the mountains of Eimeo were totally concealed beneath the lagoon, nothing would be left at sea level but a ring of coral, which, like the other atolls of the Pacific, would mark the former perimeter of a high island.

Even while he was confined to the ship on the long ocean passage, Darwin found evidence to support this theory that one reef type evolved from another. FitzRoy's charts showed that there were examples of every imaginable intermediate form, a veritable continuum from reef-fringed islands whose coral formations certainly did not stand atop a submarine crater, to miniscule islands encircled at great distances by a barrier reef, to true atolls that enclosed nothing but a deep lagoon. His confidence in the subsidence theory was only reinforced by the week Darwin spent exploring the atoll of Keeling (now Cocos–Keeling) in the Indian Ocean in April 1836. There, FitzRoy found no bottom less than two miles outside the reef despite sounding with a line 7200 feet long, which meant that the atoll probably stood atop a precipitous rampart of 'Coral limestone … of great thickness,' rather than on the shallower slopes of a volcanic cone. 'Under this view,' Darwin wrote in his diary, 'we must look at a Lagoon Isd as a monument raised by myriads of tiny architects, to mark the spot where a former land lies buried in the depths of the ocean.' Three weeks later at Mauritius, a well known depot where FitzRoy had no need to conduct any survey, Darwin went out in a boat himself to make soundings of the fringing reef. An often overlooked set of field notes shows that he repeatedly pounded the bottom with a tallow-filled leaden

> 66 *Oh the degree to which I long to be once again living quietly, with not one single novel object near me. – No one can imagine it, till he has been whirled around the world, during five long years, in a ten Gun–Brig.* 99
> To J. S. Henslow, 9 July 1836

Darwin's sections through a coral reef island

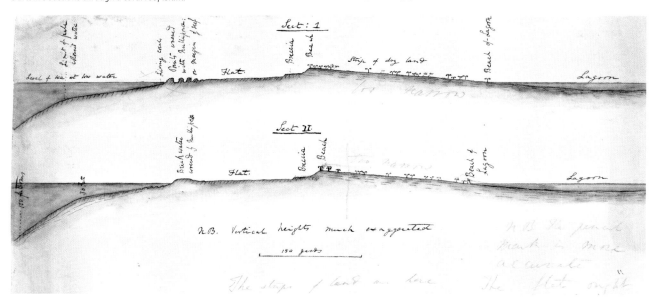

bell that took imprints of the growing corals, providing him his best evidence about the various genera that formed a reef at different depths.

After the voyage Darwin's coral theory became the key to his meteoric rise in the science of geology under the patronage of Charles Lyell. The elder geologist arranged for Darwin to present a paper to the Geological Society of London 'On certain areas of elevation and subsidence in the Pacific and Indian Oceans, as deduced from the study of coral formations,' which used Darwin's explanation of atolls to support the Lyellian principle that landforms rose into being and sank away gradually over an immensely long geological history. At this meeting, Lyell grandly renounced the crater–rim theory he had espoused in his *Principles of Geology*, anointing Darwin as a great theorist in his own right and making him Lyell's most celebrated and effective ally in the cause of gradualist geology.

Conrad Martens and his 'Beagle' watercolours

SIMON KEYNES

The Martens sketchbooks represent the artist's immediate response to scenes and landscapes encountered during the cruise which took the *Beagle* from Monte Video to Valparaiso between early December 1833 and late August 1834. When the *Beagle* reached Valparaiso, Martens would appear to have been instructed by FitzRoy to produce a series of finished watercolours, based on his pencil and watercolour sketches. FitzRoy went through Martens's sketchbooks, marking with his initials 'RF' the sketches of which he approved and in which he was interested. He selected a few of the sketches in 'Sketchbook III', made as the *Beagle* sailed south from Monte Video and into the Strait of Magellan (December 1833–February 1834); a high proportion of the sketches in 'Sketchbook I', covering the expedition up the Rio Santa Cruz in April–May 1834, the visit to Chiloé in July, and part of the time at Valparaiso in August; and a high proportion of the sketches in 'Sketchbook IV' (now in the Kerry Stokes Collection, Perth, Australia), used by Martens during the visit to Tierra del Fuego (February–March 1834), as the *Beagle* made her way from the Atlantic to the Pacific (May–June), and also at Valparaiso (July–August).

As one would expect, the watercolours made by Martens at Valparaiso represent a significant development from his pencil or watercolour sketches, not least because they are significantly larger and more carefully finished. Martens was able to take account of any notes he had written on the sketches as guidance for colour and other matters, and he was also able to 'improve' the compositions as he saw fit. For example, only a small number of his sketches include an image of the *Beagle* herself, seen at anchor from a vantage point ashore; but in several cases, where a view had been sketched from the ship as she sailed past a mountain, or stood at anchor in a sheltered bay, Martens added a ship – evidently an imaginary *Beagle* – in the corresponding watercolour, to indicate scale and to provide a focal point.

Martens left the *Beagle* at Valparaiso, and made his own way across the Pacific,

❝ You cannot imagine how curious I am to behold some of the old views, & to compare former with new impressions. I am determined & feel sure, that the scenery of England is ten times more beautiful than any we have seen . . . I am convinced it is a most ridiculous thing to go round the world, when by staying quietly, the world will go round with you. ❞
To Caroline Darwin, 18 July 1836

(Overleaf)
Conrad Martens's watercolour of Port Famine woods 6 February 1834

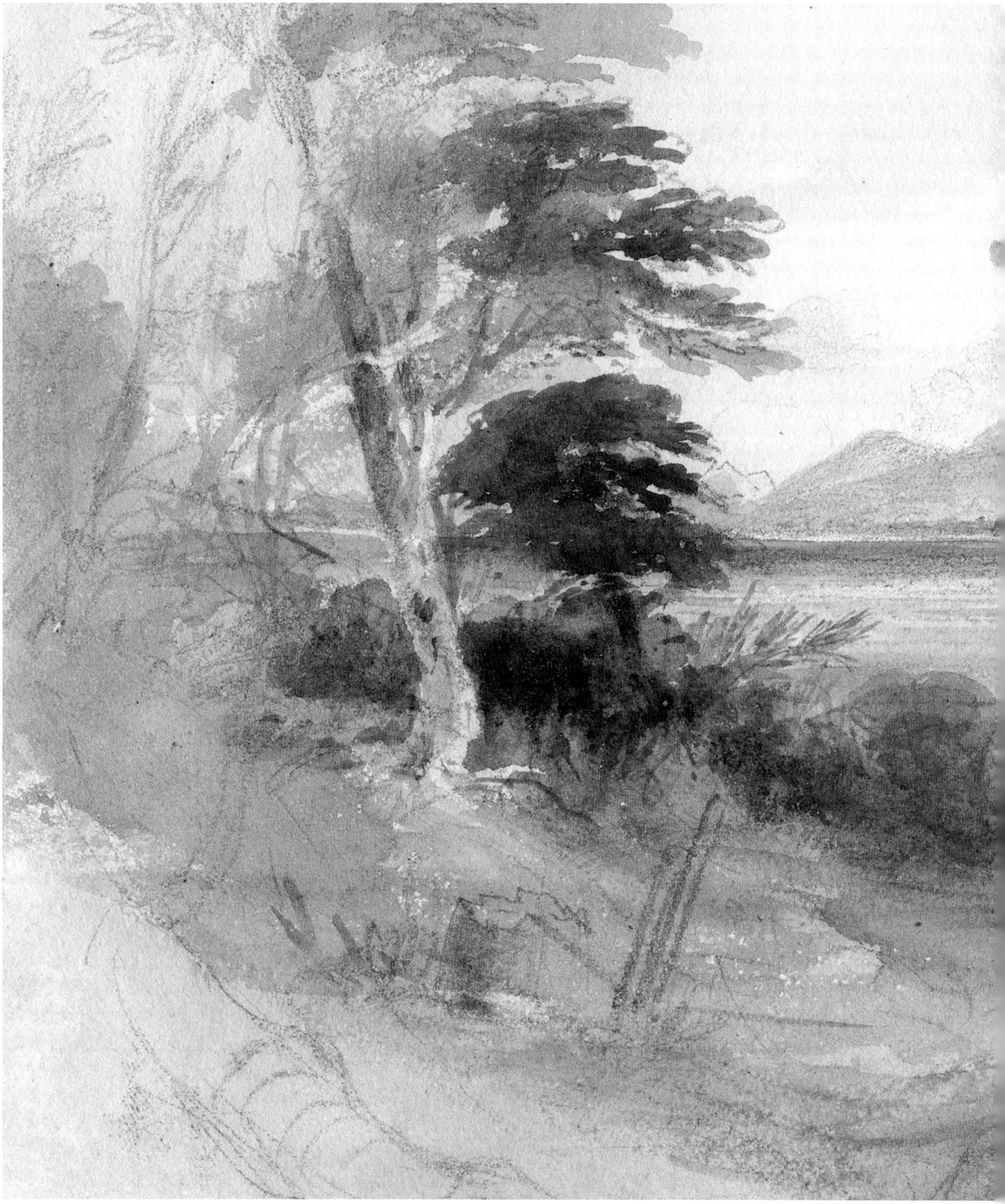

Mount Tarn ... side of ... Port Famine
Feby 6. 183[?]

via Tahiti, settling at Sydney in 1835. He had retained his sketchbooks, and continued to use them as the basis for 'Beagle' watercolours made in Australia thereafter; so, when the Beagle arrived at Sydney, in January 1836, FitzRoy and Darwin took their place among his first customers. FitzRoy commissioned a view of Tahiti ('Sketchbook I'), and Darwin commissioned a view in Tierra del Fuego ('Sketchbook IV'), and a view of the expedition up the Rio Santa Cruz ('Sketchbook I'). The two watercolours cost Darwin 3 guineas each, and hung at Down House for the rest of his life.

The watercolours made by Martens at Valparaiso became the property of Captain FitzRoy. He sent a few of them back to Francis Beaufort, to illustrate one of his reports, but kept the rest with him on the Beagle for the return voyage to England, since they would be needed for his own purposes. Several of them were engraved as illustrations for the first and second volumes of FitzRoy's Narrative (1839), with some further 'improvements'. Almost all of the original watercolours passed subsequently to his daughter Laura FitzRoy; about fifteen of them are now in the National Maritime Museum, and about thirty others remain in private hands.

Leonard Jenyns and fish identification

RICHARD C. PREECE

When Captain FitzRoy approached his friend George Peacock, then a Fellow of Trinity College, to suggest a Cambridge man who would be fit and willing to accompany him on the Beagle voyage. Peacock immediately thought of John Stevens Henslow, and of Leonard Jenyns, the vicar of Swaffham Bulbeck, who was nearly ten years older than Darwin. Both declined the offer, Henslow because he was a married man with a family, and Jenyns, after a day's hesitation, largely on account of his parish responsibilities. Both men then agreed that Darwin 'in all respects, would be a fit man to go' and so 'his name was at once sent up to Capt. Fitzroy, and the appointment confirmed'.

Jenyns had known Darwin since he was an undergraduate at Christ's College, Cambridge, but despite their difference in age, their shared passion for natural history drew them together. Jenyns noted that in those early days Darwin was 'a most zealous Entomologist, and attended but little – so far as I remember – to any other branch of Natural History'. The two went on joint excursions to collect insects in the Fens and in the woods around Bottisham Hall, near Jenyns's home. Indeed a friendly rivalry developed such that Darwin's delight in seeing his name in print for collecting a rare insect in 1829 was enhanced because he had got one over on Jenyns, who noted rather soberly that Darwin 'made a number of successful captures I had never made myself, though a constant resident in the neighbourhood'. Some of the beetles that were collected by Darwin when he was an undergraduate are currently exhibited in the University Museum of Zoology.

Jenyns may have pondered on that decision but it is clear that he was not jealous, remarking that 'no better man could have been chosen for the purpose', a testament

Leonard Jenyns

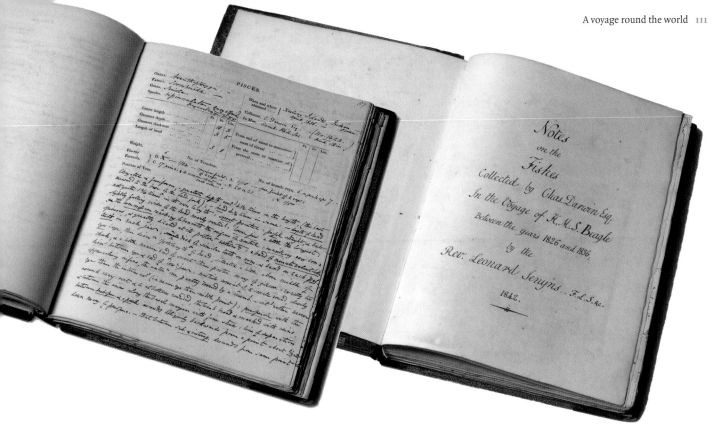

Darwin collected this specimen of the fish 'Seriolichthys' bipinnulatus *near Keeling Island in the Indian Ocean in April 1836, and gave it the field number 1423. It is a member of the caranguid family that contains the Jackfish and Pompanos.*

In his specimen list Darwin described it as 'Fish. Band on side 'Azure blue'. above a duller greenish blue; beneath two greenish metallic stripes; lower half of body snow white'

The specimen was one of those sent to Leonard Jenyns for identification. Jenyns described it in his manuscript Notes on the Fishes Collected by Chas. Darwin Esq. In the Voyage of HMS Beagle, *now in the University Zoology Museum, Cambridge, where he referred to it using the then current generic name of* 'Seriola' bipinnulatus.

'to the grasp his master mind had taken of Natural History in all its departments, and quite revolutionizing the whole science of Biology as then conceived'. When Darwin returned from the voyage there was no-one available to describe the fish that he had collected. At Darwin's request Jenyns took on the challenge, although it was not an easy one: at that time Jenyns had only worked on fish from the British Isles. He started from first principles and made detailed scientific measurements and descriptions of each new fish on his regular visits to Cambridge. He humorously commented that just the mention of Darwin's name brought on a fishy smell. This task was to be the most rigorous and exacting scientific work that Jenyns would ever undertake and culminated in the *Fishes of the Zoology of the Voyage of the Beagle* published between 1840 and 1842. The manuscript version of this survives together with many of these fish specimens in the University Museum of Zoology. This collection includes type and other specimens, which remain of lasting value for scientists.

Darwin famously became something of a recluse after his return from the voyage of the *Beagle* and Jenyns saw him 'only at intervals' but they remained in regular correspondence. Darwin's letters to Jenyns still survive in Bath, where Jenyns moved in 1850.

> 66 *Charles is come home – so little altered in looks from what he was five years ago & not a bit changed his own dear self ... his hatred of the sea is as intense as even I can wish.* 99
> From Caroline Darwin to Sarah Elizabeth Wedgwood, 5 October 1836

SIMON KEYNES

Darwin's Journal of Researches

When Darwin was a schoolboy, a friend of his had a book called *The Hundred Wonders of the World* (1818), which he often read, and which first gave him 'a wish to travel in remote countries'. A few years later, during his last year at Cambridge, Darwin read Alexander von Humboldt's *Personal Narrative* and he remarks that it was this work, together with Sir John Herschel's *Preliminary Discourse on the Study of Natural Philosophy* (1830), which stirred up in him 'a burning zeal to add even the most humble contribution to the noble structure of Natural Science'. Darwin's first contribution to this genre of literature was his *Journal of Researches* (1839); and many years later, when reviewing his publications in his *Autobiography* (1876), he remarked how the success of what he called his first literary child always tickled his vanity 'more than that of any of my other books'.

Several of those who sailed on the *Beagle* are known to have written letters home during the voyage, or to have kept journals; but far more survives for Darwin than for any other member of the ship's company. In addition to the large quantity of his scientific records, there are the letters sent in rotation to three of his sisters (Caroline, Susan and Catherine), other letters to his friends, and the original manuscript of the 'commonplace journal' he kept on board and sent home in instalments (now known as his 'diary'). During the last year of the voyage (1835–6), both FitzRoy and Darwin began work on their respective accounts, published subsequently, in May 1839, as the second and third volumes of the three-volume *Narrative*. Darwin's volume, entitled *Journal and Remarks 1832–1836*, was issued separately in August of the same year as his *Journal of Researches*. Darwin wrote in advance of its publication to Alexander von Humboldt; when Humboldt thanked him for his book, specifying eight 'beautiful pages' which contained passages offering 'the charm of a happy inspiration', how eager the author must have been to look them up.

A revised (second) edition of the *Journal of Researches* was published by John Murray in 1845, with significant alterations and additions in which Darwin began to reveal the unfolding direction of his thoughts. Following the publication of *Origin* in 1859, the *Journal of Researches* was re-issued by Murray in an improved format (1860), uniform with the *Origin*. New editions, with illustrations, appeared in 1888–90, including Murray's own most attractive volume (1890), later issues of which incorporate two of Philip Gidley King's sketches of the *Beagle*. And so it went on, consolidating and extending Darwin's posthumous reputation, and ensuring that the voyage itself is now seen essentially through his eyes.

Layout of the Beagle from Philip Gidley King's sketches of the Beagle, Journal of Researches (1890)

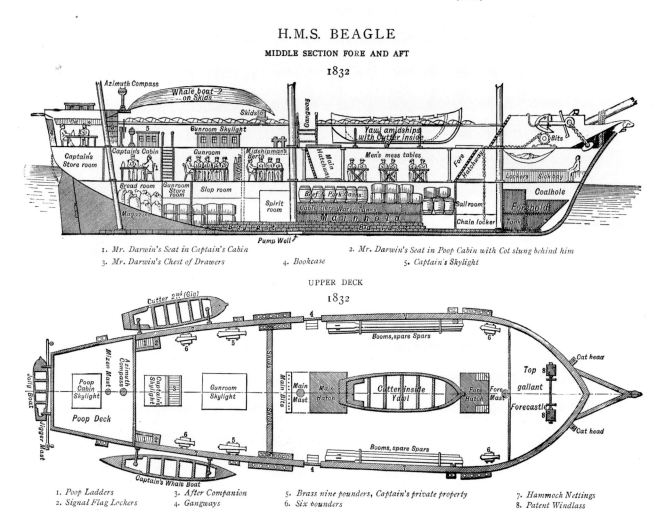

Contributors

Lyall Anderson is currently researching Charles Darwin's rock collection at the Sedgwick Museum. His background is in museum work, palaeontology and field geology. His interest in geology developed from fossil collecting in the Old Red Sandstone quarries of the East of Scotland.

Katherine Antoniw received her MSc in Science Communication from Imperial College. She is currently investigating Darwin's petrological collections from the *Beagle* voyage for the Sedgwick Museum's 'Darwin the Geologist' exhibition.

Jim Bloxam, Senior Book Conservator at Cambridge University Library (CUL), is an Accredited Conservator of the Institute of Conservation. His research interests lie mainly in the history of books; their structural qualities and their cultural context. He has conserved a wide range of material at CUL, including Conrad Martens's sketchbooks I and III. Extracts from his 1998 Honours dissertation exploring Martens's interpretation of his mandate and his concept of the activity of 'sketching' are published on the CUL website (http://www.lib.cam.ac.uk/).

Adrian Friday is at the University Museum of Zoology, Cambridge, where, until 2006, he was Curator of Vertebrates. He has had an interest in Darwin the zoologist since even before he was taught by Sydney Smith.

Candace Guite is the College Librarian at Christ's College, Cambridge. Her primary research interests are Darwin's experience of college life, and his university education in its widest aspects. She has followed Darwin from his favourite beetle hunting grounds in the Fens to a visit to the Galápagos Islands in 2008.

Shelley Innes is an editor of *The Correspondence of Charles Darwin*. She has a special interest in Darwin's barnacle work and his correspondence with German naturalists.

Simon Keynes is Elrington and Bosworth Professor of Anglo-Saxon, University of Cambridge, and a Fellow of Trinity College. He is the author of *Charles Darwin, his family, and the voyage of the Beagle* (London: Henry Sotheran Ltd, 2009).

David Kohn is Oxnam Professor of Science and Society, Emeritus, at Drew University, and general editor of the *Darwin Digital Library of Evolution*. He was formerly an editor with the Darwin Correspondence Project, and was co-editor of *Charles Darwin's Notebooks: 1836–1842*.

David Norman is the Director of the Sedgwick Museum, Cambridge University. His research is focused on the systematics, functional biology, biogeography and evolution of ornithischian dinosaurs and he has written a number of more popular books, including *A very short introduction to Dinosaurs* for OUP. He is the Odell Fellow at Christ's College, Cambridge, where he teaches geology and zoology in the Natural Science Tripos.

John Parker is Professor of Plant Cytogenetics in the Department of Plant Sciences at Cambridge, Curator of the University Herbarium, and Director of the University Botanic Garden. His experimental research concerns the genetic structure of plant populations, while his historical research examines the research programme of John Henslow, Darwin's mentor, at Cambridge in the early 19th century.

Alison Pearn is Assistant Director of the Darwin Correspondence Project, University of Cambridge, and curator of Cambridge University Library's Darwin Bicentenary exhibition 'A voyage round the world'.

Richard Preece is Senior Assistant Curator in Malacology in the University Museum of Zoology, Cambridge. He shares with Leonard Jenyns an interest in land and freshwater molluscs and is a specialist in their history during the Quaternary ice ages.

Alistair Sponsel is a post-doctoral fellow at the Smithsonian Institution Archives in Washington, DC. He studies the history of the life- and earth-sciences and is currently writing about theories of coral reef formation since the eighteenth century.

Paul White is an editor on the Darwin Correspondence Project at Cambridge University Library, and is the author of *Thomas Huxley: Making the 'Man of Science'*. (Cambridge 2003).

Acknowledgments

This book has grown out of the ideas of many people. My greatest debt is to the contributors for their time and expertise; it has been a pleasure, a privilege, and great fun to work with you. For reading the text, and for their advice and encouragement, I also thank Rosy Clarkson, Sandra Herbert, Francis Neary, Anne Secord, and Martin Rudwick – they have saved me from a number of errors and any that remain are my own fault. This book would not have been possible without the constant support of Jim Secord and all my colleagues on the Darwin Correspondence Project, and of Pat Bateson and colleagues on the Cambridge University Darwin Festival committee.

Thanks are also due to the curators of the collections who have given advice and enabled access to the material in their care, in particular Adam Perkins at Cambridge University Library, Colin Higgins at Christ's College Library, Matt Lowe and Russell Stebbings at the University Museum of Zoology, Francis Neary at the Sedgwick Museum, Gina Murrell at the University Herbarium, and Cathy Power at English Heritage. Henry Cowles helped select quotes from Darwin's correspondence.

David Kohn is grateful to Randal Keynes and, indirectly, to Thalia Grant for bringing the quote from the *Zoology of the 'Beagle'*, 3: 63 to his attention.

I am grateful to Reeve Photography and colleagues at Cambridge University Library's Imaging Services department for their time and skill; to the owners of all the collections for permission to use images, and particularly to Mr Gerard Crombie for permission to reproduce the portrait of William Darwin Fox. Everyone who works on Darwin owes a great debt to his family, and particularly to William Huxley Darwin for permission to quote from Darwin's unpublished material.

On behalf of all the contributors, I thank Stephen Bourne and Cambridge University Press for supporting this publication: I particularly thank Cathy Ashbee, Emma Baxter, Richard Marley, and Heidi Mulvey, who all at different stages have moved the project forward. And thanks to Chris McLeod of Hart McLeod who designed this book with enthusiasm, flair, and considerable patience.

And finally thank you to all those, related to me and otherwise, who have put up with the continual presence of this book over many months.

ALISON M. PEARN

Bibliographic references and selected further reading

Browne, Janet. 1995–2003. *Charles Darwin.* 2 vols. New York: Knopf.

Burkhardt, F. ed. 2008. *Charles Darwin: The Beagle letters.* Cambridge: Cambridge University Press.

Correspondence: The correspondence of Charles Darwin. Edited by Frederick Burkhardt et al. 16 vols to date. Cambridge: Cambridge University Press. 1985–.

FitzRoy, Robert ed. 1839. *Narrative of the surveying voyages of His Majesty's Ships Adventure and Beagle between the years 1826 and 1836.* 3 vols. London.

Herbert, Sandra. 2005. *Charles Darwin, geologist.* Ithaca, London: Cornell University Press.

Herschel, John Frederick William. 1831. *A preliminary discourse on the study of natural philosophy.* Published in John Lardner's Cabinet cyclopaedia. London.

Humboldt, Alexander von. 1814–26. *Personal narrative of travels to the equinoctial regions of the new continent during the years 1799–1804.*

Journal of researches: Journal of researches into the geology and natural history of the various countries visited by HMS Beagle under the command of Captain FitzRoy, RN, from 1832 to 1836. by Charles Darwin. London. 1839.

Keynes, Richard Darwin ed. 1979. *The 'Beagle' record: selections from the original records and written accounts of the voyage of H.M.S. Beagle.* Cambridge: Cambridge University Press.

Keynes, Richard Darwin ed. 2000. *Charles Darwin's Zoology Notes and specimen lists from HMS 'Beagle'.* Cambridge: Cambridge University Press

Keynes, Richard Darwin. 2002. *Fossils, Finches and Fuegians.* London: Harper Collins.

Lyell, Charles. 1830–33. *Principles of geology, being an attempt to explain the former changes of the earth's surface, by reference to causes now in operation.* 3 vols. London.

Stott, Rebecca. 2004. *Darwin and the Barnacle. London:* Faber and Faber.

For a reconstruction of the contents of the Beagle library, see F. Burkhardt *et al.* eds *Correspondence*, vol. 1, Appendix IV.

For selections from Darwin's own publications, including *Journal of Researches, Origin of Species, Decent of Man* and the *Autobiographies* see Darwin, Charles Robert. 2008. *Evolutionary writings* edited by James A. Secord. Oxford: World's Classics.

NORTH
AMERICA

ATLANTIC
OCEAN

ENGLAND
Falmouth Plymouth

Bay of
Biscay

PORTUGAL

SPAIN

Western
Islands

Cape Verd
Islands

St Paul
Rocks

Sandwich
Islands

PACIFIC OCEAN

Galapagos
Islands

SOUTH
AMERICA

Pernambuco

Ascension Island

Bahia

St Helena

Marquesas

Lima
Callao

Rio Janeiro

Low or Dangerous
Archipelago

Arica
Iquique

I. St Catharina

ATLANTIC

Society
Islands

Copiapo
Coquimbo

OCEAN

Valparaiso
Juan Fernandez
Concepcion
Valdivia
Chiloe

Santiago
Buenos
Ayres

Montevideo
Maldonado

Chonos
Archipelago

Bahia Blanca
Rio Negro

Port Desire

Straits of Magellan

Falkland
Islands

South
Georgia

Cape
Horn

Staten Island

Sandwich
Islands

New South Shetland

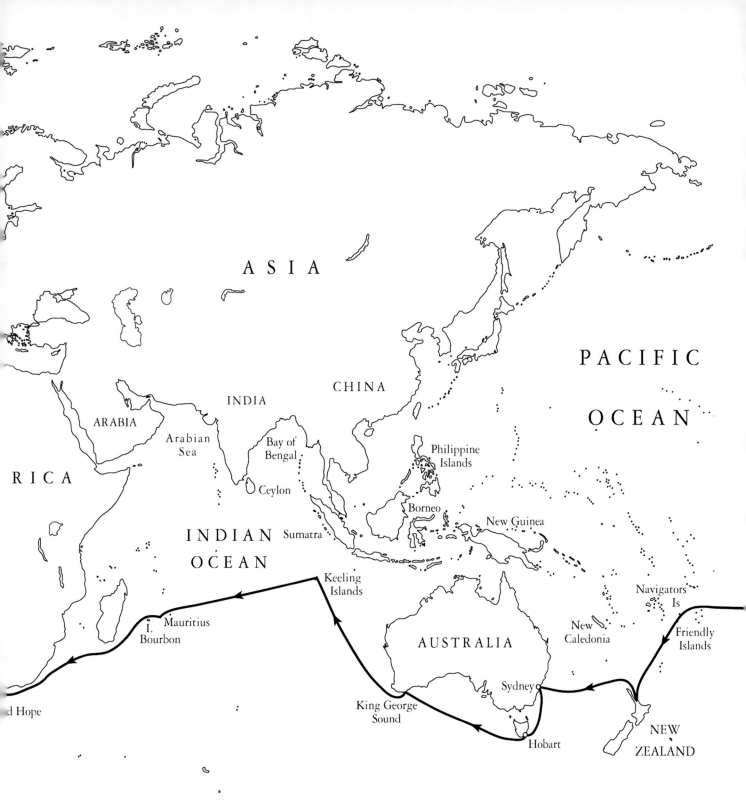

ASIA

PACIFIC

OCEAN

ARABIA

INDIA

CHINA

Arabian
Sea

Bay of
Bengal

Philippine
Islands

RICA

Ceylon

Borneo

New Guinea

INDIAN
OCEAN

Sumatra

Keeling
Islands

Navigators
Is

I. Mauritius
Bourbon

New
Caledonia

Friendly
Islands

AUSTRALIA

d Hope

King George
Sound

Sydney

NEW
ZEALAND

Hobart

The Beagle's voyage round the world

Illustration credits